12-25-92

Jan—
I hope your success story will rival these.

Ralph

A Few Good WOMEN

Breaking the Barriers to Top Management

JANE WHITE

Foreword by Elizabeth Dole

PRENTICE HALL
Englewood Cliffs, New Jersey 07632

Prentice-Hall International (UK) Limited, *London*
Prentice-Hall of Australia Pty. Limited, *Sydney*
Prentice-Hall Canada, Inc., *Toronto*
Prentice-Hall Hispanoamericana, S.A., *Mexico*
Prentice-Hall of India Private Limited, *New Delhi*
Prentice-Hall of Japan, Inc., *Tokyo*
Simon & Schuster Asia Pte. Ltd., *Singapore*
Editora Prentice-Hall do Brasil, Ltda., *Rio de Janeiro*

While great care has been taken to ensure that the information in this book
is as accurate as possible at the time of publication, the author accepts no
responsibility for any loss, injury, or inconvenience sustained by anyone using
this book. Nor is this book to be used as a substitute for legal advice on matters
of sex discrimination.

10 9 8 7 6 5 4 3 2 1

Library of Congress Cataloging-in-Publication Data

White, Jane, 1948-
   A few good women : breaking the barriers to top management / by
Jane White.
     p.   cm.
   ISBN 0-13-318940-6
   1. Women executives—United States—Interviews. I. Title.
HD6054.4.U6W46 1992
658.4'0082—dc20   92-10228
                                                  CIP

ISBN 0-13-318940-6

PRENTICE HALL
Professional Publishing
Englewood Cliffs, NJ 07632
Simon & Schuster, A Paramount Communications Company

Printed in the United States of America

DEDICATION

This book is dedicated to my husband, Bruce; we could use a few more good men like him.

ACKNOWLEDGMENTS

I'd like to thank the following people for their invaluable assistance: Patricia Michael, formerly of the National Association of Female Executives, for providing me with some great source material; Brad Carr of the New York State Bar Association for being the nicest wisecracker I know; Vicki Tashjian of Wick & Co. for her input and insight; and attorneys Maryann Saccomando Freedman, James Heller, and John Rapoport for their expertise on discrimination law and patience with my lack of it. Last but not least, my heartfelt thanks to the 15 women profiled in this book for their courage and commitment toward making the working world a better place for all of us.

FOREWORD

The courageous women profiled in this book are part of a "quiet revolution"—a revolution which has seen women enter the workforce at an astonishing rate in the past several decades.

But despite this growth, who among us can say that discrimination against women has disappeared? Who among us can doubt that a woman, no matter how well-schooled or how golden her resumé, enters many business organizations with limited or no hope of reaching the top?

For the fact is that any overview or examination of the makeup of the American workforce finds women—and minorities—reaching plateaus from which they feel they cannot climb. For example, *Fortune Magazine* recently studied 800 of the largest U.S. companies. Of the 4,012 people listed as the highest-paid officers and directors of these companies, only 19 were women—that's less than one half of one percent.

Additional evidence of the presence of what has been called the "glass ceiling" can be found in a recent survey of the nation's 1,000 largest corporations by Korn-Ferry and the UCLA Anderson Graduate School of Management. This study revealed that minorities and women, who today account for more than half of the workforce, hold less than 5 percent of top managerial positions.

In an effort to help act as a catalyst for change in management attitudes and policies, in July 1990, as Secretary of Labor, I launched my "Glass Ceiling Initiative" to investigate the ways senior management positions are filled and whether minorities and women were being developed for such opportunities. Specifically, we examined training, rotational assignments, developmental programs, and reward structures—all the indicators of upward mobility in corporate America.

While I was Secretary, I heard from many companies who were already taking positive steps to dismantle their glass ceilings. Several companies developed tracking systems for identifying and developing high potential minorities and women for their workforce. Others have now asked executive search and recruitment firms to make an extra effort to include minorities and women in their candidate pools.

Let me make it clear: The glass ceiling initiative had nothing to do with quotas, and everything to do with equal opportunity. I do not believe that the role of government is to mandate who private enterprise should hire for specific positions. Rather, I wanted to issue a "wake-up call" to American business, telling them in no uncertain terms that if they effectively block half of their employees from reaching their full potential, they're only hurting themselves.

In the next decade, fully two-thirds of new entrants into the workforce will be women. The bottom line is simple. If employers want to compete in today's complex global market, then they can't afford to discriminate. They can't afford to ignore the needs of working women. Employers who do will simply lose out to those who don't. And, in the final analysis, America will lose out.

I was struck—but not surprised—by the fact that many of the trail blazers portrayed in *A Few Good Women* stress the importance of mentors. As a young woman in my twenties working for a United States Senator from North Carolina, I sought out the advice of Maine's Margaret Chase Smith, who was regarded by many as the "conscience of the Senate." I don't know how many U.S. Senators would share an hour with a 22-year old total stranger seeking advice. But Margaret Chase Smith did, and she recommended that I bolster my education with a law degree.

This experience left me with a keen sense of responsibility to be available for young women who are in need of a mentor. My door is always open to them—and I hope your doors are open, as well.

I have always taken heart from the words of a woman who conquered incredible challenges. Unable to see or hear, she never ran for office, never raised a family, and never entered the job market. Yet she inspired millions.

"One can never consent to creep," said Helen Keller, "when one feels an impulse to soar."

Through the leadership of women such as those profiled by Jane White, I am confident that the "glass ceiling" will meet the same fate as the Berlin Wall, and that all women who enter the workforce will be able to soar as far and rise as high as our skills and talents will take us.

Elizabeth Dole
President, American Red Cross
Former U.S. Secretary of Labor

TABLE OF CONTENTS

PART ONE

Women in Management:

Such a Long Way, Baby?

chapter 1

DISMANTLING THE 10 BIGGEST MYTHS ABOUT WORKING WOMEN

This book is dedicated to the proposition that while all women are created equal, some had the benefit of better parenting.

Some "experts" on women and management perpetrate the myth that there are sex-linked differences in management style based on the assumption that *all* women had cookie-cutter "feminine" upbringings—were taught never to use profanity, talk out of turn, smoke nonfilter cigarettes, or exceed the speed limit. These so-called experts legitimize the practice of *safe sexism* by proclaiming that because of these distinctions, women will never be admitted to the fraternity of management because men don't feel comfortable around them. But, as a consolation prize, women can resign themselves to biology's control over their destiny and use their female attributes—their tendency to "nurture," "listen to others," and "build consensus"—to carve out their separate-but-equal niche in the workplace.

A Few Good Women does not treat women as if they were a second sex, or a separate-but-equal sex, but as individuals who come to the management playing field with everything it takes to make a top flight CEO. It's the playing field that's booby-trapped, due to "attitude problems" on the part of certain of their male coworkers, subordinates, or bosses; men who aren't used to seeing women in any other role in society other than helpmate.

None of the eleven women executives profiled in this book were raised by their parents to "nurture," "listen to others," or "consensus-build." They were encouraged instead to excel, think on their feet, compete, and lead. Many of these women were raised and influenced by working moms and grandmoms, and therefore entered the workplace unencumbered by the psychological baggage of feeling unworthy of success, or guilt about leaving their own kids with somebody else.

Many of them had parents who treated them as equals to their brothers—encouraging them to make things with their hands, to excel at technical subjects such as math and engineering, to debate ideas at the dinner table, to compete in sports—pursuits that lay the foundation for their success in the working world. By the same token many of these women (like some men in business) also feel no shame in taking no interest in sports, since they've sought out work environments where their on-the-job contributions are valued more highly than the ability to grouse over a myopic umpire's calls.

Because these women were raised in "equal opportunity" environments as little girls, they were encouraged to think of boys not only as equals but as friends and confidants. That outlook lay the groundwork for feeling at ease with male colleagues as adults, whether manifested in going out for a beer with the guys after work or talking shop. Not surprisingly, these women also selected husbands who shared their egalitarian outlook—as well as the housework-load on the "second shift."

Therefore, it should be no surprise that this book does *not* make a big issue out of sexual harassment. It's not that I downplay the severity of the crime, I simply do not believe that sexual harassment is the primary problem that professional women face. At least one workplace survey backs me up: a 1992 poll of more than 1,000 working people by the Roper Organization found the majority reporting "no" or "not much" sex harassment at work.[1]

The problems facing professional women, women in management especially, are not that men use their power to intimidate women. The problems occur when the balance of power has shifted so that it's the woman who is now "on top," and some men can't reconcile this relationship with their images of women as either subordinates or helpmates.

What's more, the media did more harm than good to the image of professional women in the aftermath of Professor Anita Hill's accusations against Supreme Court nominee Clarence Thomas by depicting the workplace as a battlefield where the men are the victors and the women their helpless victims. This characterization is fair neither to working men nor women. Most women in the workplace don't assume either that men are the enemy or that women are helpless victims of such immature behavior; therefore, when confronted with such behavior, these women take action.

"Sometimes a woman can solve the problem by herself," attests Melanie Kirkpatrick, a writer for the *Wall Street Journal* who earlier in her career walked out on a date with an editor at a different newspaper who was harassing her. "The cops don't have to be called out every time."[2]

What's more, frequently the woman's male colleagues are the ones who "call the cops" because they recoil at this unseemly conduct as well. Construction industry executive Kathryn Gray reports that in a situation where she was harassed at work it was her male colleagues who were outraged and rushed to her defense. Because they were "not anxious to lose a good worker (me), they brought it to the attention of my boss" and the harassment stopped. Gray adds that women such as Anita Hill who 'play the victim' are "an affront to other professional women who have succeeded in establishing clear parameters in the workplace so that women can succeed and prosper in male-dominated organizations."[3]

The problem faced by professional women is that some men in the workplace feel that *they* are the victims of nature gone awry when the woman is in the position of authority and power and the man is the subordinate. Men react to this perceived violation of nature the only way they know how—through *denial*—they try to downgrade the women to their notion of women as wives: they ignore them, discount them, patronize them. As Betty Lehan Harrigan put it in her trenchant *Games Mother Never Taught You* (Warner Books, 1977), when men can't distinguish women from waitresses, daughters, or cleaning ladies, "their thinking is muddled and their game goes to pot." This is when the real problem for professional women begins. Unfortunately many men in the workplace, unlike the often *extra*ordinary women who comprise the majority of female executives, were products of *ordinary* upbringings, whose stay-at-home Moms were perfectly content to fry up the bacon rather than bring it home, who dutifully picked up their dirty underwear, drove them to Little League, and deferred to Dad.

Relating the experiences of eleven of America's most successful female executives, who work in established industries ranging from computers to broadcasting to manufacturing, *A Few Good Women* reveals the inside scoop on how to be treated as an equal—or a superior—and not a wife. In many cases, these workplace frustrations are what MIT professor Mary Rowe calls *microinequities*, behaviors that can make it difficult, if not impossible to do your job but that aren't defined legally as "actionable" acts of discrimination.

Specifically, these female executives advise readers:

- How to spot a problematic boss—and trade him in for a new one.
- How to react to men who don't acknowledge your brilliant idea in a meeting—but amazingly incorporate that very same idea into their own anyway.
- How to deal with a subordinate who won't get his work done because he resents reporting to a woman.
- How to cope with male clients who won't take you seriously.
- How to use *authority words* to demonstrate your power to skeptical males outside of your realm of authority—whether they're outside vendors or managers of other departments.
- How to fend off male clients who want to mix business with pleasure—and still make the sale.
- How to respond if you're asked to take notes in a meeting—even if you're a peer with the other participants in it.

I hope this book will succeed in helping women break through the "glass ceiling" that seems to bar them from the CEO's suite, and at the same time, I want to send a message to CEOs across the country who are asking themselves, "What DO women want, anyway?" What women want, Mr. CEO, is simply a level playing field in the workplace; not separate-but-equal accommodations.

Myths I'm Destroying in This Book

Here are 10 myths about working women that I help destroy in this book:

Myth #1: Women don't have what it takes to be in top management because they don't possess "management skills"—an attribute which is inherently male and learned only through male bonding rituals such as team sports and fraternity initiation rites.

The truth: If women can run countries, they can run companies—and we all know Margaret Thatcher never needed any assertiveness training! The only reason why you can count more females at the helm of ships of state than as captains of industry is because of the selection process involved; the first is democratic, the second autocratic.

Myth #2: Women can climb the corporate ladder by possessing that amorphous quality known as "leadership skills" *or* by **"working twice as hard as a man."**

The truth: Given the cutthroat competition among the massive baby boomer population for a shrinking number of management jobs, women aren't going to go anywhere in the workplace merely by being workhorses or yes-women. They have to work smarter than men. That means distinguishing themselves by receiving advanced degrees or professional certification or by developing the technical competence to excel in industries that value these attributes—for instance, the computer industry. Of the eleven women "near the top" profiled in Part Two in this book, four are CPAs, two are lawyers, three have MBAs and six work in the computer industry.

The other way for women to get noticed is by establishing a reputation within their companies as problem solvers, often by taking assignments others spurn. Some of these women transformed money-losing entities into profit centers or created new profit centers, as did five of the women profiled in this book: Sara Westendorf of Hewlett-Packard Co., Nancy Faunce of Eastman Kodak Co., Shirley Prutch of Martin Marietta Corp., Carlene Ellis of Intel Corp., and Linda Wroblewski of Richard Eisner & Co.

Myth #3: You can get ahead at a company on merit alone without having a mentor.

The truth: It's a rare woman whose talents are so prized by the company that they're sufficient to propel her to the top. Five of the women profiled—Nancy Faunce, Karen Reimer of Honeywell, Jacquie Arthur of M/A-COM Inc.,

Carlene Ellis and Loraine Binion of Levi Strauss & Co.—all acknowledge being helped by a mentor, who either assisted them in "breaking the glass ceiling," or brought them into the company "over the ceiling" from the outside.

The converse is true, too: if your mentor leaves the company you may have no ally in the event of a restructuring or a downsizing, as Nancy Faunce found out when Kodak eliminated the unit she headed up and she found herself virtually having to beg for a job. Furthermore, if you can't find a mentor, become your own—as did Melissa Cadet of River West Developments (profiled in Chapter 9).

Myth #4: You can get ahead at a company by being a "good girl," keeping your nose to the grindstone and your mouth shut despite the fact that your boss is sabotaging your career, on the assumption that a powerful magic prince in the company will notice that it's your foot that fits the glass slipper.

The truth: If you don't take charge of your career and find a boss that recognizes and rewards you for your talents, your career is in deep trouble. Nine of the 11 executive women featured in this book either had to change bosses within their companies, leave the company, or threaten to leave it in order to improve their job situations.

Myth #5: All women are equal.

The truth: Unfortunately, a significant percentage of working women think that the most they can accomplish in life is to stroke the ego of a successful man, as opposed to getting by on their own ideas. Unfortunately, these women often get promoted over competent women by male bosses who regard them as wife-surrogates. We call this genre of women *eraser-clappers* because they get ahead by playing teacher's pet.

Myth #6: Creating quotas will solve the problem of too few women in top management. Many companies try to "do the right thing" for their female employees by pressuring managers to promote a certain percentage of women to a certain rank within a given time period.

The truth: Although it is a well-meaning practice, the creation of quotas can lead to a disproportionate number of eraser-clappers (see Myth # 5) getting promoted and an alarming number of competent women being forced to look elsewhere for work.

Myth #7: Most working moms feel guilty about working.

The truth: Of the eleven executives profiled in this book, five were raised by working moms or grandmoms and wouldn't have had it any other way. What's more, of the five executive women profiled who *are* working moms, none of them professed guilt feelings about leaving their children in the hands of a competent caregiver. So those companies who pander to the portion of the workforce made up of guilt-feeling Moms by offering corporate day care not only aren't being sensitive to so-called "women's issues" but they're sending a dangerous message to other employees that executive mothers don't really have their hearts in the right place: the workplace.

If there is a "day care crisis" it centers around the fact that most working mothers don't earn enough to afford two-career amenities such as live-in nannies, carry-out meals, and cleaning services that would ease their workload on the "second shift"—since the average female college graduate in America earns the same salary as men with only a high school diploma. Solution: close the pay gap.

Myth #8: It's possible to rank companies on how "friendly" they are to women employees.

The truth: These rankings typically examine whether a company offers on-site day care and extended maternity leaves as a barometer of enlightenment, rather than whether the company promotes women or offers them training in line responsibilities such as sales or manufacturing, or offers them overseas assignments. As even Lorraine Dusky, coauthor of *The Best Companies for Women*, admits, even companies with "terrific benefits for maternity leave had a glass ceiling so low that you couldn't stand up straight without bumping into it."[4]

What's more, the folks doing the ranking of companies often treat job titles such as Vice President of Public Relations or Human Relations as if they were fast-track jobs, when in reality this track never leads to the destination of a CEO's office. For example, an otherwise authoritative directory published by the now-defunct *Business Month* entitled "100 Women to Watch in Corporate America" (June 1989) contained no less than 28 women in what insiders derisively call the *Pink Ps*—personnel and public relations. These women will *not*, contrary to *Business Month*'s assertion, "figure to make serious runs at the highest posts."

Myth #9: Men are the enemy.

Many so-called experts on women in the workplace assume that the two sexes speak a different language, so that the only way a woman can communicate with men in the workplace is to speak more shrilly. But six out of the eight married executive women profiled name their husbands as their number one mentors, not only serving as their cheerleaders but for the most part agreeing to put their own careers second. If these men are the enemy, who needs friends? What's more, not only is there a supportive husband in the wings behind many successful female executives, but there's usually a terrific male boss ahead of her; the guy who was gutsy enough to go to bat for her despite the less-than-enlightened outlook of other men around him. Which leads us to . . .

Myth #10: Barriers keeping women from top management will be cracked eventually, we just need more time.

The truth: We need more courageous men, not just more time. The reason for the existence of the "glass ceiling"— the phenomenon that women seemingly can't go any higher than middle management—isn't that women haven't been in the job pipeline long enough to deserve to see the light at the end of it. There have been plenty of deserving female executives who have been in the workforce since the late 1960s and early 1970s and therefore have paid their dues when it comes to accumulating "time and title."

The seeming discrepancy between the large number of women in lower-management and supervisory jobs and the tiny number in executive or officer-level jobs has more to do with the amount of courage on the part of the people doing the choosing than it does the tenure of the women seeking and deserving to be chosen.

Let's face it, it's relatively "unrisky" to promote a woman to a supervisory or middle management slot where she need only win the cooperation of her subordinates. It's quite another matter to give a woman a high-stakes post in charge of sales, or mergers and acquisitions—and risk losing the company revenues because a client or acquisition candidate simply won't do business with a woman. Two of the women profiled in this book, Karen Reimer of Honeywell and Melissa Cadet of River West Developments, cited difficulty winning the cooperation of clients as an important barrier faced by women climbing the corporate ladder.

Yes, the barriers will fall in corporate America but we'll need our "few good men" who have shown exceptional courage in recent years to exhibit some extraordinary courage in the years ahead by putting women in visible positions.

The Good News: We Are Making Progress

Some of the pressure against the barriers will come from outside the corporations themselves. Three important developments have led to a healthy chain of events promoting equality in the workplace: a milestone lawsuit, a federal edict, and favorable demographics, all of which will influence the likelihood that we'll see a significant number of women "manning" the podium at annual shareholders' meetings in years ahead. Here are just a few links in that chain.

First, the lawsuit: the landmark Supreme Court decision in May 1990 ordering the Price Waterhouse accounting firm to make management consultant Ann Hopkins a partner of the firm has put other consulting firms on notice that they can no longer behave like a private club when it comes to selecting people to join the elite inner circle of partners. The fact that Hopkins was a top performer at the firm also destroyed the myth that men don't promote women because men think women can't do the job, since Hopkins was apparently doing it better than any of the other candidates for partner.

The most significant effect of the Hopkins victory is that it has given millions of women across the country the self-confidence to stop blaming themselves when they confront "attitude problems" on the part of their bosses and the courage to take action—whether that means filing a lawsuit or simply finding a more enlightened boss or employer.

Here are some examples:

- Frances Conley, a professor of medicine, resigned from Stanford University medical school in the summer of 1991 after 16 years, charging "gender insensitivity" on the part of male colleagues. Among other affronts, Conley cited being called "honey" in the operating room by other surgeons, or "on the rag."

    Conley said the incidents had been going on for her entire 25 years as a surgeon but she didn't talk about them sooner "because in order for a female to get taken into the club . . . you have to become a member. Had I made an issue of some of the things that were happening during the time that I was a resident, I wouldn't have gotten to where I am."[5]

- In September 1991, a California jury awarded $6.3 million to a woman employee of Texaco Inc. who sued after she was twice passed over for a promotion. The award is being touted as the largest amount ever awarded in the U.S. in a sex discrimination case.[6]

- Attorney Ingrid Beall, an expert in tax and international corporate law who has practiced at the same firm since 1958, charged her employer, Baker & McKensie, with sex discrimination in a lawsuit filed in October 1991. Beall [demonstrated that it's not always enough for a woman to shatter the glass ceiling!]: she was a partner in the firm but charged that the other partners were hoarding all the lucrative work. Beall said that her income fell 64 percent over a three-year period because she was denied assignments.[7]

The second important landmark for women in the workplace followed quickly on the news of the Hopkins decision; the announcement by then-federal Labor Secretary Elizabeth Dole in August 1990 that she intended to bring down an EEO-style enforcement mechanism on companies that weren't promoting women to the top jobs. And, like it or not, when some CEOs heard her sabres rattling, they very likely hustled to change their management makeup out of sheer terror that they might have to contend with such a mechanism. While this reaction might appear to be the right kind of progress made for the wrong kind of reasons, it's better than no progress at all.

The third important development, the changing demographics of the workplace, will be a constant theme in the years ahead. Not only will there simply be more women in the workplace according to predictions by the Bureau of Labor Statistics, but many of these women are the daughters of the male CEOs, CFOs, and COOs of today who have the power to change the makeup of tomorrow's management teams. And, thanks to the achievements of the courageous and tenacious women who have gone before them, these up-and-coming female executives *expect* to be treated fairly in the workplace, they don't just hope for it. And if Dad doesn't do right, he'll hear from them.

chapter 2

WOMEN ON THE CORPORATE LADDER: SO NEAR, YET SO FAR FROM THE TOP

In *Megatrends 2000* John Naisbitt named the 1990s as the decade of women in leadership. He's optimistic about the role of women in the workforce. For one thing, they're ubiquitous: As he points out, women without children are even more likely to work than men in that category—79 percent versus 74 percent.

In many professions women have increased from a minority as low as 10 percent in 1970 to a critical mass ranging from 30 to 50 percent. Naisbitt also points to the growth of *Working Woman* magazine, which at a circulation of 900,000 in 1988 is surpassed only by *The Wall Street Journal* among business publications.

If you're looking purely at labor force participation, Naisbitt is right. The number of women joining the ranks of certain professions has certainly mushroomed over the last three decades. The population of female lawyers and judges has skyrocketed from 7,500 in 1960 to more than 180,000, female doctors from 15,672 to 108,000, and female engineers from 7,404 to 174,000.[8]

The demographic makeup of institutions that provide the imprimatur for success in business has changed as well. In the 1950s, women made up only 20 percent of college undergraduates in contrast to 54 percent today, and two thirds of them dropped out to get their "Mrs" degree instead of holding out for their BA.[9]

Consider when Harvard University first grudgingly accepted women to its business schools in 1959: While they were allowed to attend class with their male peers, these women had to sit in the back and take their exams at Radcliffe College.[10]

The gray eminences at Harvard would have a tough time finding enough room in the back of the class for females if they tried to enforce that practice now: Women now account for 27 percent of MBA students, compared to 4 percent in 1972. In the same time period, the percentage of women at Stanford's B-school has mushroomed from 2 percent to 33 percent, and at Columbia from 7 percent to 32 percent.[11]

But these numbers only tell half the story. They reflect the fact that the expectations of women have certainly improved; women expect to pursue a college degree and they expect to be successful in the workplace. However, when you start measuring statistics reflecting success—i.e., the numbers of women in top management—you're no longer measuring expectations but acceptance. And unfortunately, most men don't want women in the club.

Consider the fact that there are only three CEOs of Fortune 1000 companies: Katharine Graham of the Washington Post Company (and she got a head start, inheriting the business from her husband's dad), Linda Wachner of Warnaco Group, Inc., and Marion Sandler of Golden West Financial Corp.

Okay, we admit it, there are only so many CEO jobs to go around. But you don't see a lot of female COOs, CFOs, or even executive VPs, either. Among Fortune 500 companies, only 1.7 percent of corporate officers are women, according to a 1986 study by Mary Ann Von Glinow, a professor in the school of business at the University of Southern California.

The magazine that invented the term Fortune 500 came up with similar findings. When *Fortune* magazine examined 1990 proxy statements of 799 of the top public companies it found only 19 women listed among the highest paid officers or directors—or less than one half of 1 percent.[12]

Minority women have it tougher. Black females made up just 2 percent of managers in companies with 100 or more employees in 1988, compared with Black men, who accounted for 3 percent of this group and white women, who totaled 23 percent, according to the latest data available from the Equal Employment Opportunity Commission.[13] Not one Black woman was among the top 25 Black managers in corporate America when *Black Enterprise* magazine ran an article naming them in 1988.[14]

Being a "twofer" helps some minority women get a foot in the door of a company, but not a leg up on the corporate ladder, as you'll discover in reading the chapters profiling Loraine Binion and Melissa Cadet in this book.

"Being a twofer doesn't give you legitimization, doesn't give you a voice or power and doesn't move you up," contends Ella Bell, a University of Massachusetts professor who is studying more than 100 Black and white women managers in companies throughout the U.S.[15]

Studies of how far women have moved up within individual professional specialties—banking, the media, law, and accounting—also produce dismal findings.

Women in Banking

When several pioneering New York City businesswomen opened The First Women's Bank on Park Avenue in 1975, somebody showed up with a picket sign saying, "A woman's place is in the home, not in the bank."

The bank came close to bankruptcy after the deregulation of the industry in the early 1980s and was finally acquired by a group of investors in 1987. With new capital of nearly $30 million it began thriving, but at the expense of its early ideals. Now called The First New York Bank for Business, it has only two women on its 27-member board.[16]

Women who attempt to break into management at established banks haven't fared so well, either. According to the American Bankers Association, women make up a whopping 75 percent of the banking work force, but fewer than 8 percent of senior management. Although women hold 41 percent of the middle-management jobs in banking, they seem to plateau at this level.[17]

An informal survey of the 10 largest banking companies in the United States, conducted in March 1989 by *The Los Angeles Times*, found only three women out of more than 200 senior executives with titles of Executive Vice-President or its equivalent. None of the major American banks has a woman CEO.[18]

Pam Mollica, Vice-President/Treasurer at Clinton Savings Bank in Worcester, says, "there is definitely a glass ceiling in banking . . . where are the women at the top?"[19]

The reason why more women aren't "manning" the till? Some observe that women couldn't even get into management training programs at big financial institutions 20 years ago, when the grooming would have to start. Women pursuing careers in banking during the 1960s and 1970s were slotted into staff spots in personnel and corporate communications—the "velvet ghetto" that functions as a comfortable coffin instead of a way-station to power.

Some women who were smart enough to get on the right track from the beginning, however, feel that ambitious women need more than time on their side if they want to break through the glass ceiling in banking.

For example, Patricia Jones began her career right out of college as a bank teller at a time when business schools didn't welcome female MBA candidates. After her first promotion she was right where she wanted to be—in the lending department where line officers are groomed.[20]

Then Jones moved to Mechanics Bank in Worcester, Mass., where she worked her way up to Assistant Vice President and Trust Officer. During this time, she earned an MBA, attended the Bank Marketing Association's basic training school for senior bankers and took management courses at the Tuck and Wharton business schools.

All the right moves, right? Not if you're the wrong sex. Jones says she stagnated in the AVP slot, watching a man get promoted over her who had no MBA and no more experience. She finally left the industry in 1986 to open an accounting firm.

Funny thing about glass ceilings, they often are visible only to those banging their heads against them. In a survey of male CEOs and female vice-presidents, Financial Women International learned that 71 percent of the women believe there is a glass ceiling and 73 percent of the men don't think there is.[21]

Putting the question another way produced the same disparity: Asked whether women have the same career opportunities as men, 49 percent of the men said yes compared with 18 percent of the women.

"There is definitely a gap between reality and perception," says Polly DiGiovacchino, President of the group—not to mention a gender gap based on which sex is doing the perceiving. "It's up to male CEOs," she adds, "to close it."[22]

Women in the Media

The media is another sector that may give "equal time" to political candidates of opposing views but doesn't treat opposite sexes equally. A study conducted by Victoria Fung for the Gannett Center for Media Studies at Columbia University contends: "Women still form a kind of underclass at the networks, where men's salaries run anywhere from 15 percent to 81 percent higher, where an unwritten double standard requires female anchors to be an average of 20 years younger than male anchors and where looks often matter more than experience and credentials."[23]

Women in Law

There may be plenty of "lady lawyers" peopling the set of *L.A. Law* and grabbing media headlines at the local prosecutor's office, but don't look for their names on the shingle. While about one in three associates of a law firm is a woman, only one in 13 is a partner, according to Carrie J. Menkel-Meadow, a professor at the University of California at Los Angeles.[24]

"Even assuming an ever-increasing lengthy time to (attain) partnership, the number of women partners is still much below what it would be predicted to be," says Menkel-Meadow.

The American Bar Association did its own study of the profession, which came up with different numbers, but still isn't much more encouraging. It says only 20 percent of all lawyers are women and 8 percent of the partners at large law firms are women.[25]

Women in Accounting

A report issued in 1987 by the American Institute of Certified Public Accountants found that sexism is still a bar to advancement in the field. And the numbers bear that assessment out: Only about 3.7 percent of the partners at major accounting firms are women.[26]

"The accounting firms are only now coming to the conclusions that women are as capable as men," says Arthur Bowman, editor of *Bowman's Accounting Report*.[27]

Some people say that the numbers will change as more women move up the ranks. Women now represent an impressive 50 percent of the nation's accounting majors in college and half of the recruits at the major blue-pencil firms. As recently as 1983, only about 25 percent of accounting majors and 20 percent of new recruits were women.[28]

Women in Education

What boggles the mind is that even in the realm of academia— the "accepted" environment for women—the numbers are just as dismal. According to the American Association of University Women, although approximately two-thirds of all public school teachers are women, only 5 percent of the nation's superintendents are female. They hold a miniscule number of college and university presidencies; fewer than 350 of the nation's approximately 3,000 institutions of higher learning are headed up by women.[29]

Excuses, Excuses

Naturally, people who observe management trends can offer plenty of reasons why women aren't making it to the top, most of which don't stand up under scrutiny.

Some explain the relative dearth of women in top jobs by contending they haven't been in the career pipeline long enough to deserve to emerge from the end of it. Not true, says Judy Mello, 46, who was CEO of First Women's Bank in New York City in the early 1980s: "My generation came out of graduate school 15 or 20 years ago. The men are now next in line to run major corporations. The women are not. Period."[30]

In fact, there were already 100 women executives who were on the fast track to the top as far back as 1976, according to *Business Week*.[31] But when the magazine revisited them 11 years later, not one of them held the top spot in a public corporation (unless they inherited the position or started the business).

What's more, of the 46 women that *Business Week* tracked down in 1987, only 16 stayed at the same company and only one left to start a family—which also contradicts a lot of the media hype about how most working women opt to stay home with the kids if they have to choose between family and career.

Speaking of working moms and hype, two studies published in early 1990 revealed women quit their jobs at a higher rate than do men *not* because they've been derailed on the "mommy track" but because they come from the wrong side of the gender tracks. A study by Wick & Co., a Wilmington, Delaware consulting firm, showed that of women professionals who quit their jobs, 73 percent left to work for other companies, 13 percent started a business and 7 percent were looking for new jobs. Only 7 percent left to go home.[32]

"Not one of the women in our study mentioned that she was leaving to obtain better benefits such as maternity leave or day-care assistance," says Victoria Tashjian, Vice-President of Wick.[33]

When asked if there was anything going on in their personal lives influencing their decision to quit, women mentioned children only 9 percent of the time—even though two thirds of the women in the Wick study had children. Interestingly enough, the men in the study mentioned children 26 percent of the time.

A separate study released in 1990 by Opinion Research Corp. of Princeton, N.J., echoes the same sentiment. Data gathered on more than 26,000 male and female managers, supervisors, and professionals at seven big service and manufacturing corporations revealed that women managers were more likely than men to say they intended to leave their company within the next year. Women were also more dissatisfied than men with their career development.[34]

"Compared to male managers, female managers perceive that they have fewer opportunities for advancement and less chance of achieving their career objectives in their organizations," the study concluded.

Getting to the Top: What's the Answer?

So how do we get more women in the top jobs? With a federal edict? Quotas? Corporate consciousness-raising sessions?

On the federal edict front, then-Labor Secretary Elizabeth Dole announced in July 1990 that she was devising a "glass ceiling initiative" to try to speed the promotion of women and minority members to top posts, threatening cancellation of government contracts with companies that didn't cooperate.[35] Labor Department officials say female, Black, and Hispanic employees make up 30 percent or more of the middle management of big corporations, but less than 1 percent at the level of CEO and vice president. To discourage practices that limit careers, Dole said, "we will be examining developmental programs, training, rotational assignments and reward structures—all the indicators of upward mobility in corporate America."

But as the women profiled in this book demonstrate, at this rarified level of corporate life, discrimination against women is typically subtler than the overt obstacles to hiring and promotion that show up at lower levels. Executives may be favored for promotion if they have completed a "tour of duty" in a foreign assignment, for example. And let's face it, it's a lot easier for a stay-at-home wife to play the role of trailing spouse than a husband with a high-powered career.

Unfortunately, less than four months after she announced her glass ceiling initiative, Dole resigned from the cabinet to become President of the American Red Cross. (Of course, some pundits say she is preparing for a run for the White House, in which case she can carry out her glass ceiling objectives as the "CEO" of the administration rather than as a bureaucrat in the government's version of the human resources department.)

In the meantime, the torch has been passed to Dole's successor, Lynn Martin. In August 1991, Martin released the department's glass ceiling study of 94 companies, which found that women only occupy 16.9 percent of management positions at all levels and just 6.6 percent of executive level jobs.[36]

Focusing on nine unnamed companies, the DOL's Office of Federal Contract Compliance identified "systemic barriers" for advancement and created a prototype to use in future investigations. While none of the companies surveyed, including PepsiCo. Inc. and Sterling Drug, were found to be technically discriminatory, they did break some rules.

The barriers included the following:

- Instead of hiring from diverse labor pools, as affirmative action and EEO regulations require, company management relied on word-of-mouth referrals.
- Bonuses, perks, and favorable performance reviews were most frequently given to white men.
- Not enough effort was made to give high-visibility, career enhancing assignments to women and minorities.

The DOL's Office of Federal Contract Compliance plans to "negotiate corrective action" in companies that violate these rules. The Office, which initiates investigations rather than waiting for complaints, has a potent (if rarely used) ultimate weapon: the debarment of government contracts if discriminatory practices aren't changed. In 1990 it found discrimination in about 25 percent of the cases it took on.

How successful the initiative will be is anybody's guess. Periodically, businesses prepare legal challenges to the OFCC mandate and to affirmative action itself, arguing that these are de facto quota incentives.

Women's groups hope that the DOL will put its enforcement power where its mouth is and take action against those companies who are found to be discriminatory and don't take action to mend their ways. "If all that's done is a report, it will be a great disappointment," says Marcia Greenberger, president of the National Women's Law Center in Washington, D.C.[37]

In the meantime, how do you get companies to run more like meritocracies than autocracies or fraternities? Some companies are waking up to the fact that, like it or not, many of the freshly-minted college graduates they'll be recruiting in the next decade or so will no longer be the "new boys" that they can groom to be "old boys."

Corporate executives will be faced instead with what demographers call the *diverse workforce*, the fact that the share of women in the workforce, along with people of African, Hispanic, Asian, and Native American origins, will rise while the white male share of the labor force will drop to 39.4 percent by the year 2000 from 48.9 percent in 1976.[38] By the year 2000, the number of Black women in the work force is expected to total 8.4 million, up from 6.5 million in 1987, while the number of Hispanic women is projected to increase to 5.8 million from 3.4 million, according to Harbridge House, a Chicago consulting company.[39]

So companies that are sensitive to the diversity and demographics of the new labor pool are preparing their employees for that eventuality now.

Women-Friendly Companies

While most of the programs to advance women in companies are more window-dressing than substance, there are still some businesses who are making an outstanding effort. For example, Kentucky Fried Chicken created a program in 1989 called *Designate*, whose aim was to attract and keep female and minority group executives. "We want to bring in the best people," says Kyle Craig, President of Kentucky Fried Chicken's U.S. operations. "If there are two equally qualified people, we'd clearly like to have diversity." The program is achieving noteworthy results: While in 1989 none of the company's 17 senior managers were minority or female, in 1991, seven were.[40]

KFC finds candidates for its Designate program by retaining search firms owned by minority members and women as well as by white men. Armed with the same criteria, each recruiter is asked to produce a different slate of candidates: all white men, all women, or all Black men. One person is hired from each search. Of the 13 people who have been brought in under the program, two are white women, two are Black women, three are Black men, and six are white men.

At Chubb Inc., a Warren, N.J. insurer, women have constituted an impressive 50 percent of entry-level professionals hired between 1982 and 1990. Although progress has been made, most of them are still bunched up in the middle ranks with only a few of them bursting out of the pipeline into more senior-level positions.[41]

"Something is happening in that 10-to-12-year development process where the playing field gets less level," says David Fowler, Chubb's Senior Vice-President and Managing Director.

One strategy, Fowler said, is to hold managers accountable for how they advance women and minorities and publish these results in quarterly "at-bat reports" which affect bonuses.

"Those branch managers who fill 30 jobs with white males bat zero, and those who fill a bunch with women and minorities get hits."

Corning Glass Works has made a commitment to find out why it can't hold women down on the farm. "We do a good job at hiring but a lousy job at retention and promotion," says CEO David Houghton. At Corning, one in seven female employees left between 1980 and 1987, double the one-in-fourteen rate for white males there.[42]

In 1987, Houghton warned male executives that their own promotions would depend in part on how well they helped women and minorities "reach their fullest potential."

Corning's male managers also imbibe a dose of consciousness raising. In groups of about 20, they have been attending one-and-one-half day workshops to explore sexism in the workplace. One male manager in one of these workshops confessed to believing that women who have babies quit to raise them. He was surprised to learn that 75 percent of women who left to take maternity leaves returned after eight weeks.

Beware of "Experts" on Working Women: Not All Experts Are Allies

Many people are confused about what working women really want. During the last decade we've all been bombarded with the message that in their heart of hearts, working women would rather be at home raising kids, a notion that thankfully was dispelled partially by the Wick study reported above.

The legitimization of the notion of the schizophrenic working woman, torn between career and kids—or what we call "safe sexism" practiced by so-called experts on the workplace—has probably done more to sully the positive image of women in business than any backward attitude manifested by a male manager.

Among the leading practitioners of safe sexism is management consultant Felice Schwartz, who generated well-deserved controversy in 1989 by recommending in the *Harvard Business Review* that there be two tracks for women—a fast track for the strictly career driven and a slow one for women who want to balance career and family.

Schwartz claims that she was misunderstood, but we think the lady protested too much in the heat of the ensuing controversy. For example, in defending her choice of a medium to convey her dual-track message, she let slip her low opinion of her constituents: "I wanted the *Harvard Business Review* because I wanted to reach corporate leaders," she told a newspaper reporter. "This was not an article for women. I did not write the article for *Good Housekeeping, Ms.,* or *Working Woman.*"[43]

Felice Schwartz is certainly not the only "expert" on working women who is giving women a bad name, however. The practitioners of "safe sexism" whether in the form of management consultants or advice-book authors, also defame women by legitimizing the notion of women as the second sex; that they have a distinct "management style" that emphasizes "nurturing," "building consensus," and "empowerment" while men are better at being leaders.

Not surprisingly, it's this very simple-minded stereotyping of women that has relegated them to the soft, fluffy pink ghettos of human resources and public relations instead of being put in charge of running factories, leading sales teams, and heading up mergers and acquisitions departments.

Perhaps the most insidious threat to the image of women comes from the so-called "experts" on women, the self-styled, self-fulfilling prophets of doom who conduct highly unscientific surveys that are gobbled up by the media, who need see only an authoritative report validating the existence of three swallows to be convinced it's summer. Journalist Susan Faludi defrocked some of these snake-oil selling gurus in her excellent book, *Backlash* (Crown Publishers Inc., 1991), citing:

- the "surveys" by Yankelovich Clancy Shulman reporting that 30 percent of women believe that "wanting to put more energy into being a good homemaker and mother" was reason enough to quit a job
- the shoddily researched 1986 *Fortune* cover story entitled "Why Women are Bailing Out," never offered supporting statistics to its assertion
- the "research" by "women's expert" Srully Blotnick claiming that unmarried women were so desperate to get hitched that their spinsterly misery ended up damaging their careers.

Even *Savvy*, a short-lived business magazine aimed at working women, did its own bit to discredit ambitious working women in a 1986 article entitled "Falling Off the Fast Track." First of all, the advice from *female* headhunters was that women should ask their bosses for the reasons why they were fired so that they could "learn" from them. (Can you imagine that conversation!) The article went on to cite a study conducted by the Center for Creative Leadership that asked 22 male executives (talk about a small sample!) to discuss "women who had not lived up to management's expectations." The researchers found three main reasons why these women derailed:

- They wanted too much power. They were too overt about wanting a top job.
- They had a performance problem.
- They were unable to fit in. (Although the study admits that these women couldn't get any feedback from superiors to find out why.)

The article also referred to another study by Srully Blotnick (whose credentials as a psychologist, even his degree, turned out to be fabricated) which virtually labeled ambitious women as frauds: Blotnick claims that he was told by male executives that women fail because "They don't really want to do the work, they just want the rewards immediately. They're all sizzle and no steak."

Nowhere in this article was the "other side of the story" presented; that the women may very well have derailed from the fast track not because they were exceeding the speed limit but because they were "pushed." While the report tells us nothing about women, it does reveal plenty about the mindset of the 22 male executives queried. Too ambitious? How many men with this character trait similarly didn't measure up to their boss' yardstick for success? As for the women that "didn't fit in," the logical question should have been, fit in to *what*? To these male manager's preferred image of women as soft, fluffy deferential helpmates?

"Did you hear me?" The Communication Gap Between Men and Women at Work

Probably the most difficult task ahead is to get men who may not take their wives' ideas seriously to treat women in the work-place differently—whether these women are their subordi-nates, peers, or bosses. One of the most frustrating workplace dilemmas confronted by the women profiled in this book is that men don't listen to them; or they'll "hear" what a woman will say in a meeting without acknowledging the idea and amazingly—almost subliminally—that idea will turn up later in their own thoughts.

In paying homage to the end of Margaret Thatcher's reign as Prime Minister of Great Britain, journalist Janet Daly noted that one of Thatcher's unsung contributions to humanity was getting men used to the idea that women have ideas of their own.[44] Daly recounted her own encounter with a man with this particular conceptual handicap in the *London Independent:* "I remember a dinner at which I sat next to a man . . . who spent most of the evening holding forth around and through me on various topics, addressing his remarks to the men at the table while scarcely meeting my eyes.

"Eventually he began to expound on a subject on which I had considerable amount of expertise. An embarrassed col-league looked gallantly in my direction and said that he had read a paper of mine on that very subject. At this, my neighbor turned to me and gaped as if he had just been told that the cat was about to play Beethoven's Violin Concerto."

Daly is not the only woman who has had to contend with being the invisible woman in the company of deaf men. For example, despite all the progress that has been made admitting women to universities in the past 20 years, male professors seemingly have difficulty seeing their raised hands from behind the lectern, according to a study by researchers David and Myra Sadker of American University. The Sadkers found that professors typically call on women students less frequently than men, make eye contact less frequently, ask women less challenging questions, and don't wait as long for their answers.[45]

In a separate study, the Sadkers suggest that women are already programmed to think of themselves as second class citizens long before they enter college. The couple found that elementary school teachers, as well, most of whom are women, tended to have greater expectations of their male students. For example, when boys called out for attention, teachers would accept the remarks as contributions but girls were told to raise their hands, the researchers found. What's more, when students need help, teachers will give boys direction but will tend to do the girls' work! Lastly, the Sadkers observed that teachers tend at the same time to praise and criticize the boys more.[46] The upshot: boys are taken more seriously.

Not surprisingly, women themselves find it difficult to take the ideas of other women seriously, suggests a study by University of Delaware psychologist Florence Geis, who observed the reactions of 168 men and women to female speakers and found that audience members of both sexes were more likely to frown or furrow their brows at female speakers and to smile and nod approvingly at men.[47]

Perhaps the best example of women not being heard is manifested in at least one of the reactions to the Wick study mentioned above: the revelation that most women work because they want to, just as men do, and quit jobs because they want challenges, not to be home with the kids. But some men still don't "get it." Philadelphia printing executive George Clement told a *New York Times* reporter that he's finally learned a lesson about why it's wrong to define job satisfaction differently for women than men after he made an unsuccessful attempt to hold onto female employees by offering them flex time.[48]

Now he thinks he knows why women *really* want a fulfilling job: It's "to compensate for how awful they feel when they leave their children in the morning."

By George, you haven't quite got it. But that's okay. We'll keep educating you until you do.

chapter 3

WHY SO FEW GOOD WOMEN?

As I demonstrate in the next chapter, many women are "called" to join the ranks of their fellow professionals in banking, accounting, law, and other specialities but few are chosen to smash the glass ceiling and enter the inner circle of top management. When I began my search for executive women I had high hopes of featuring 15 or 20 such role models in these pages who would compare battle scars and share war stories as well as success stories in their quest for the top.

My hopes were dashed—not because my thesis proved wrong but because of the apparent vow of secrecy required by corporate America of even its high-ranking employees regarding the inner workings of corporate life—a vow that's tantamount to a loyalty oath.

In developing the criteria for selecting the successful women included in Part Two, I established three ground rules. First, the women had to be singled out for recognition as successful executives, either by having climbed the corporate ladder to impressive heights by an early age or considered CEO material by their peers. Secondly, they had to share my belief that women face gender-based obstacles in the workplace and agree to talk about how they overcame these obstacles. Thirdly, they had to be willing to "go public" by agreeing to have their names and company affiliations published along with their stories, since anonymous interviews generally lack credibility.

Finding fast-track women was easy. The now-defunct

Business Month published an authoritative list of 100 fast-track women: "Women to Watch in Corporate America" in April 1989, which was the source of six of the 13 women interviewed: Shirley Prutch of Martin Marietta Corp., Karen Reimer of Honeywell Inc., Sara Westendorf of Hewlett-Packard Co., Jacquie Arthur of M/A-Com Inc., Phyllis Swersky of AICorp, and Carlene Ellis of Intel Corp.

Crain's New York Business produced another list in its January 29, 1990 issue entitled "Forty Under Forty," profiling "40 outstanding New Yorkers who've made their professional mark before the age of 40." This list produced Richard Eisner & Co.'s Linda Wroblewski and MTV's Sara Levinson.

The National Association for Female Executives, a New York-based professional organization for women in management, was the source for three more profiles: Melissa Cadet of River West Developments, who is the president of NAFE's Sacramento chapter, Levi Strauss' Loraine Binion, who was honored by *Ebony* Magazine as one of the 100 Best and Brightest Black Women in America; Kodak's Nancy Faunce, who was nominated for *Inc.*'s Entrepreneur of the Year in 1990.

Why did I have to go to so many sources to find enough good women to profile? Because I got such a high rate of rejection from those I approached, not a reaction one would expect from women who otherwise should have been champing at the bit to have their shot at "15 minutes of fame." The first category of naysayers—the smaller category, thank God—were women who insisted that there is no sex discrimination in the workplace. A typical response would be: "Sex discrimination? Nonsense. Why, I got here, didn't I?" or "Perhaps sex discrimination exists, but I don't pay attention to it. I just keep my nose to the grindstone."

Neither of these responses stands up to scrutiny. As for the first, the I-got-here-didn't-I reaction, the truth of the matter is that an impressive title is not necessarily evidence that a woman has made it on merit, but more often that she is a beneficiary of a de facto "quota system" that affords women fancy handles but no responsibility as a way of making the company look "sensitive." As for the second response, women who either make excuses for a corporate culture that is hostile to women or who deny it or sanction it are refusing to be part of the solution and therefore are part of the problem.

Social scientists have a word for this particular mindset

on the part of these women: they call it *collusion.* According to
Marilyn Loden and Judy Rosener in *Workforce America!* (Business One Irwin, 1991), women who refuse to acknowledge that
sex discrimination exists, "shift the . . . focus away from finding productive solutions to serious problems by denying the
very existence of the problem. As such, collusion through denial
is an effective way of stalling and derailing group effort aimed
at change."

For the most part, women executives whom I approached
welcomed the premise of the book with open arms. The major
sticking point, the one that accounted for the largest group of
"dropouts" from the field of interview candidates, was their fear
of having their identities attached to their ideas because of
potential reprisals from their employers.

One of the first tip-offs that an interviewee would ultimately drop out from the roster would be this reaction: "Let me
ask my public relations department if I can participate." My
heart would sink, knowing, as a former journalist, what the
response would be. After all, the *raison d'etre* of corporate PR
departments is damage control, even in the absence of damage.
Naturally, the PR departments would deny the women permis-
sion to participate because of the perceived attendant negative
publicity. But the gag orders weren't always handed down to
control negative information but to limit the flow of *any* information to a "designated spokesperson" for the company: the
head of it. For example, one of the women who had already been
interviewed dropped out after she changed employers and learned
that only the CEO of the company could be quoted by the press
on any topic.

In my mind, it's this patriarchal top-down restriction of
freedom of speech that goes to the very heart of what's dys-
functional in corporate culture in America today and why the
workplace environment continues to be hostile to women even
in these ostensibly enlightened times more than two decades
after the birth of the women's workplace-equality movement.
The censorship occurs because, as Eastman Kodak's Nancy
Faunce puts it, the company becomes so large and impersonal
that it's "bigger than the people who work for it"—the super-
structure seemingly takes on an identity more significant than
the very individuals who give the company an identity, who
create its products, who develop its markets, and who are responsible for its profits.

One of the few beneficial effects of the debate over sexual harassment following the Anita Hill allegations is that it lifted the PR department-controlled shroud of secrecy from corporate culture and therefore pricked the bubble of its aura of legitimacy. The specter of such infantile, X-rated behavior on the part of a male executive made featherweights of those management experts who heretofore had been painting the male power elite as a paragon of decorum and dignity that women ought to emulate.

But the Anita Hill revelations nonetheless distorted the nature of the disease of corporate culture into a cartoon of a lascivious boss chasing his terrified female underling around the desk with his tongue—or other organ—hanging out. And that's not the true picture of the problems between the sexes in the workplace today. The accurate image, more often than not, isn't macho *Playboy*-reading man versus timid *Ladies Home Journal*-reading woman/victim. It's the *Sports Illustrated*-reading rather-be-fishing man whose comfortable spot in the hierarchy is threatened by the busting-her-buns *Wall Street Journal*-reading woman.

But there's a more vital reason why we need some *glasnost* in corporate America than because it exposes "unfairness" to women. American business has to come to grips with the fact, as did the hapless Mikhail Gorbachev (albeit too late) that if you cloak a crumbling empire in secrecy and terrorize those who dare to speak out against it, the end result will be defections on the part of those you muzzle and you'll be left without enough of the talent you need to fix the empire.

The reason why we need to be vigilant about treating women and other members of the diverse workforce with the respect they deserve is not to promote some warm, cozy, mooshy-gooshy we-are-the-world notion of egalitarianism. We need to do it because by denying the "different folks" a crack at running things, corporations are committing a crime against change, not mere discrimination. We need to bring in more "outsiders" to corporate America so that these newcomers, unencumbered by hidden agendas and calcified habits, can utter the naked-emperor truth about the flaws in the companies—and thereby give companies the means to solve their problems.

It's no coincidence that the most creative Americans and also its highest wage earners are its recent immigrants, the folks newly arrived to our shores who aren't yet jaded about the incredible opportunities awaiting anyone who wants to be somebody in the United States, even if these are folks with nothing in their pockets but talent and drive. As author James Fallows puts it in *More Like Us*, immigrants are "disproportionately entrepreneurial, determined and adaptable, and through history they've strengthened the economy of whatever society they join."[49] More often than not women view themselves as recent immigrants to the workplace too, having been freed from the tyranny of the apron strings that bound them to unpaid menial labor and second-class citizenship—who aren't just marking time in the workplace but feel privileged to make a lasting, tangible contribution to it.

It's not surprising then that the state of California, which is at the same time an incubator for brilliant high-tech entrepreneurs and a melting pot for minorities, is the home address for four of the 12 successful women profiled in this book. Fallows observes in *More Like Us* that California is more "American" than other states, contrasting the unbridled optimism that most Californians exhibit about their opportunities with that of their counterparts from the staid, old-money-dominated more-like-Europe Northeastern states. Californians believe "that people can learn to do things they haven't done before, can take on identities they hadn't had, can will themselves into stations in life different from those in which they were born."[50]

Patricia Johnson, who is a Vice President of Blue Cross of California and a minority woman, seconds this notion. "California companies are very sensitive to diversity because our population is changing so rapidly before our very eyes: the mix of people, the color of people, the language they speak," said Johnson, an Ohio native. "But a more important reason for the openness is that everyone is so new to business here. You don't have some of the mental barriers to new ideas that exist in the east or the south where those in power have for generations run their businesses in an old-boy manner. There are more entrepreneurs here, people who are doing their own thing in a very small way or a very large way."

The bottom line: some of the individuals who are going to make corporate America great again aren't exclusively people with white skins, one-syllable last names and wing tips. So that's why we need some of America's white male power elite to recognize that to avail themselves of some of the best ideas in the workplace they need to stop ignoring or patronizing some of the most talented people in their midst, even if these people don't walk, talk and "quack" like their wives.

PART TWO

*T*he View From

11 Women Near the Top

chapter 4

Karen Reimer
of Honeywell, Inc.:

JUST DON'T CALL HER 'HONEY!'

"That's a pretty impressive title, honey!" Hearing the "H" word from the man on the other end of the phone sent shivers up Karen Reimer's spine and her hands went clammy, but she carefully calculated how to handle this potential client's not-so-subtle sexism. Women like Reimer who have made it close to the glass ceiling have learned along the way when to let issues of gender slide and when to get tough about them.

Karen Reimer is the Director of Corporate Transactions for Honeywell, Inc. She is among a handful of women in the country who have the power to decide whether or not management's interest in buying or selling a company or subsidiary is a prudent one or fraught with peril. A quick study, she negotiated more than 10 deals in her first two years at the $7.2 billion computer giant, including the sale of its semiconductor business and one of its defense units.

"I've been told that I can take a set of documents on a company's business and finances and analyze it very thoroughly and very quickly—and there is a premium on speed and being thorough in these deals. I can save Honeywell money by avoiding some transactions that are bad deals because the acquisition candidate may have hidden liabilities on its balance sheet. Or I may conclude that it's a dandy of a company and that if we don't buy this company somebody else will."

It's an impressive position and impressive talent, one that

many men find hard to believe belongs to a woman. Many men, including the one on the other end of the line that day.

Reimer admits that when she heard the 'H' word from this fellow, her back went up. "I was frosted by that remark!" But she also bit her tongue rather than retort with a tart: "I'm sorry, you must have misheard me, My name isn't Honey, it's Karen."

She says she chose to keep silent because what was at stake was not just defending her ego but possibly affronting somebody who could make a difference to Honeywell's bottom line—whether or not the man deserved to be affronted.

Also, the remark didn't catch her off balance. For the past 10 minutes, the caller, who represented a potential purchaser of one of Honeywell's businesses, had been abruptly rebuffing her questions about his financial position. Questions that required candid answers, Reimer said, "because if he were going to buy a $100 million dollar company, he damn well better know where to find a hundred million dollars." Reimer said that she decided to inform the man of her title "so he wouldn't think I was just asking nosy questions."

"The problem is that if this guy actually has a hundred million dollars and Honeywell has no other buyer for this company then I've got to play his game. If he's got money and he's a good buyer for this company, I've got to deal with this nonsense.

"Don't get me wrong, I'm going to try and make people like him play by my own rules. But since I'm in a buying and selling game, to some extent to play that game we have to put up with all sorts of folks, including some real animals who don't realize that the women graduating from colleges these days are every bit if not more qualified to do their jobs than the men are."

Gaining Acceptance from Clients and Winning Their Respect

Reimer says she's become sufficiently attuned to the warning signs of Neanderthalism in the business world that she's honed a strategy to preempt this behavior, either by making it clear to outsiders where she belongs in the corporate hierarchy or by bowling them over with "authority words"—buzzwords intrinsic to the dealmaking process that only an insider would know.

Executive women such as Reimer recognize that when the male ear "hears" an elevated job title for a woman, the male mind downgrades the title to fit his notion of the kind of work women usually do—rather than elevating the status of the woman to fit the title.

"When these people find a woman who is in a fairly high position they assume that the woman doesn't deserve the position, that it's a 'gimme' job. They therefore assume that you don't know what you're talking about. That's happened to me a zillion times.

"For example, when I was talking to a New York investment banker recently who is representing a company in a sale to us, he'd keep asking me questions like 'Well, is there anybody else that I should be talking to at your company?' These guys try to place you in the hierarchy: they'll do subtle things like ask for organizational charts to find out where you fit."

Once alert to these verbal red flags, Reimer employs a variety of conversational gambits any woman can translate to her own industry to demonstrate her familiarity with the inner workings of the game. Reimer tells how she handled one such conversation with an investment banker.

"I went into certain details about issues that would come up during the course of the negotiation just to convince him that I've cut my teeth and have been through the process before. I always mention the length of time it will take to undertake 'due diligence' and the fact that Honeywell uses a 'discounted cash flow method' to value companies. It's always good to throw in some transaction-specific terminology—for example I'll say, 'we'll have to have a Hart-Scott-Rodino antitrust review with the Department of Justice' before the deal can go through."

"I also told him that I would take care of all necessary approvals within Honeywell. I make sure that he is very aware that I am not overstepping my bounds, that if he's sold the idea to me, he's sold it within the company."

While this belabored exercise isn't the most savory of activities—it's about as ego-enhancing as enduring a job interview with each and every potential transaction candidate—Reimer can see why it's necessary. "As much as I don't like it, his attitude is understandable on one level: He'd be mighty ticked off if he went down the road with me for two months and found out I wasn't the person he was supposed to be talking to. Then he'd have to start over and 'resell' the deal to somebody else."

A Woman With a Mission: To Smash Gender Stereotyping

Not only is Reimer sensitive to the way men view women in the workplace, she views herself as a woman with a mission at Honeywell to "create role confusion" as she puts it, educating others that women can be bosses and men can have clerical jobs.

She has more power than the average employee to do this; she also supervises five departments of the company. As part of her "mission," she hired a man as receptionist of the executive offices.

"People expect a woman to fill the job of receptionist on the executive floor," says Reimer. "And I hired a male to do that. Despite the fact that he was the most qualified candidate for the job, I still find myself in the position of having to defend the decision to hire him because it wasn't the 'traditional' hiring decision."

"I like the idea of having men hired in jobs that are typically female jobs or females in typically male jobs so that people are sufficiently confused about roles that they don't assign roles to anybody any more."

And it's not just people in the workplace who need a good dose of cognitive dissonance when it comes to roles, but their kids as well, Reimer says.

"Think about little kids who call their daddy or mommy at work and a man answers the phone. Well, pretty soon they're going to figure out that it's okay if a man is a secretary. Attitude change has to start when people are young and not when they're adults."

Helping Other Women Up the Ladder

Reimer also recognizes that a good measure of career success for women derives from being in the right place at the right time, so she does everything in her power to manipulate those two dimensions in favor of women who are farther down the ladder than she is.

"There are a lot of woman doing good work that isn't recognized because it has to 'come up through the channels.' So if I see exceptional work, rather than just 'pass up the product,' I'll tell the woman to come along with me and explain her negotiation strategy or financial analysis at a meeting where she can get noticed."

Reimer's zeal to make the workplace a better place for women doesn't stem from her own career frustrations but a deep-rooted conviction that she has an obligation to help other women. "You reach a point in life when you decide that even if life has been good to you, if other women are encountering difficulties you have a responsibility to try to change their situation."

Reared for Success

Reimer's parents inadvertently prepared her for living by her wits in the corporate world by teaching her to think on her feet as a child—"acting as her own counsel" as it were—rather than relying on them for direction.

"When I was small, I often observed that the parents of other kids would intervene on their behalf in tough situations. But if I had a problem, my parents pretty much encouraged me to solve it, they didn't intervene to solve it. My parents developed in me a tremendous sense of personal security.

"I can remember a discussion with a friend's mother about whether I could stay overnight at her house and my friend decided her mother would take her side. While I don't remember anything about the argument, I do remember my parents decided that it shouldn't be two mothers talking about the issue but me being involved on my side. Whether or not I prevailed in the discussion, they wanted me to solve these problems myself.

"And I think that's important. Because I look at it now and think if I behaved that way as a five-year-old or seven-year-old it gave me the foundation to face similar challenges as an adult, only this time I'm taking on a male executive in a corporation, not someone else's mother."

Reimer's favorite game as a little girl wasn't playing house or dolls, it was playing "office."

"We had a big screened-in porch in our back yard and Mom let me take Dad's papers and put them in different little compartments. And I can remember my father being very angry at me once because when I was playing office I was "mailing things" and I took an old insurance bill that he had paid and put it in the mail box."

When it came to crystallize in her mind exactly what kind of office game she'd be playing as a grownup, Reimer's inspiration came from watching the Watergate hearings on TV as a teenager.

"As I watched the hearings, what impressed me was the way people could influence other people just by asking questions. That's when I first decided that I wanted to go to law school."

Sidestepping Career Roadblocks

After graduating with honors from Bethel College in Kansas in 1976, she went on to get her J.D. from the University of Nebraska. Reimer joined Control Data Corporation in 1980 straight out of law school and was made staff attorney in 1983.

The reason why she decided to switch to Honeywell two years later wasn't to avoid bumping a glass ceiling but taking a sidestep around a career roadblock that confronts men and women alike: individuals higher up on the corporate ladder who are comfortably ensconced in their jobs—too comfortably.

"The term for these individuals at Control Data was *blockers*," Reimer said, "that is, somebody in the position ahead of you whose job you need to have before you can advance; there's no career path that goes around it. That somebody—male or female—is not going to be promoted but the company's not going to kick him out, either; he's there for the rest of his career. So a blocker is somebody who stands in your career path, not maliciously but inertly."

For her first three years at Honeywell, Reimer worked in the legal department, in the office of the General Counsel. At this point, Reimer ascertained that to go anywhere in a corporation you have to broaden your experience, and therefore your expertise. "During that time it was apparent that they appreciated my work, my talents, my everything, but that was what they appreciated. They weren't going to be real aggressive about broadening my career path, they just saw me as an efficient machine."

"At that point I was doing more work in mergers and acquisitions than I was in the traditional finance and securities area. So when an opportunity presented itself for me to 'lateral' into the mergers and acquisitions area, I took it. The legal department is great, but you're going to be simply doing legal work. In going into the mergers and acquisitions area you can be not only a lawyer, you can be a tax person, an accounting person, a human resources person—you have to have a little bit of knowledge about everything."

She was promoted to Director of the unit in 1988 and since then her boss, who is Vice-President of Corporate Services, has heaped additional duties on her shoulders. In addition to her M&A responsibilities, she also oversees the administration of the company's fleet of cars and trucks—the ninth largest in the United States.

Reimer admits that these duties entail much more breadth than her job title implies. But she's not hankering for a fancier handle. For one thing, "Honeywell isn't big on titles, we aren't like the banking community where virtually everybody who isn't a bank teller is a Vice-President. In any event I'm not interested in titles personally—I want significance out of a job."

However, much as she might disparage those professions where impressive titles seem to carry more weight than skill and competence, Reimer grudgingly admits that a fancier handle might help short-cut some of the verbal parrying she has to engage in with skeptical or hostile outsiders.

At the Negotiating Table: Handling Male Egos

Thus far the thorniest challenge to Reimer's authority occurs at the negotiating table itself: during the down-and-dirty face-to-face wrangling with lawyers or managers of other companies over what's a fair price for a corporation or its subsidiary.

The kinds of issues that will be sticking points during a negotiation, no matter which gender is doing the dealing, will boil down to money. "It's usually some element of purchase price, some element of financial consideration. It can be 'No, we don't have to lay off those 20 people, you have to do it.' Or, 'No we don't want to have to pay to clean up the environmental problem, you have to do it.' Or 'No, we won't take the risk on that particular program, that stays with you. You got yourself into that mess. We'll buy your business but you worry about how that program turns out.' "

Reimer recognizes that bruised egos are inevitable in the buying and selling game; nobody enjoys learning that their managers are overpaid or that their units are overstaffed. But the news is doubly hard to swallow if the messenger of bad tidings is a female. Because the reaction of the other party to a female messenger is frequently: Call in a new messenger.

"The hostility manifests itself this way: 'Look, it's tough enough for me to 'eat' the fact that I had a $400,000 salary before and now I'm going to have to take a $100,000 salary. But don't have some woman tell me that I'm going to have to take that. It's tough enough to swallow these downgrades. But don't let me have to take it from her."

"Or, let's say I'm putting some ultimatums on the table in a sell situation, stipulating actions that must be taken before the deal can go through. I might be saying to the other party that wants to buy, 'We are not going to sell this business unless you pay this general manager 'X' because otherwise he has told us he is going to quit. The other party might essentially answer me, 'If the CEO tells me that I have to do this, I'll buy it—but if you tell me, I don't know if I believe it.' "

In these high-stakes facedowns, a hostile male negotiator who thinks that women with impressive titles have "gimme" jobs with unimpressive responsibilities doesn't just present a challenge to her ego, he can sandbag the deal altogether. In the heat of the battle, Reimer has twice been forced to "call for reinforcements." She will literally bring in a male "alter ego" who will make an identical proposal on the purchase or sale of a unit that she has been making—but the hostile party will swallow it because a man is saying it.

"We typically bring in a lawyer from an outside firm to

assist on the larger deals anyway. So in one particular case where I felt I wasn't making much progress, my approach was: 'Let's have this issue resolved by our respective counsel. My reasonable lawyer and your reasonable lawyer will meet in our absence to find a solution.' And that's a way of deflecting that kind of hostility. I'll have an alter ego talk to him and I'll just feed the guy words. If he can't swallow something because it's my idea, then let it be somebody else's idea.

"It's a horrible way to have to face the issues but if a problematic person doesn't work for your company, it's not within your control to change a person who isn't ready for equality. If women are going to succeed in the corporate world they have to be bright enough to recognize that there are things over which they have no power, that you can't remake the world in a moment. So the best approach to it is to play their game— but by your rules."

How She Handles the Glass Ceiling at Honeywell

It's precisely because of the high level of resistance to executive women by the male players in the M&A game that Reimer is dubious that she'd ever be a candidate for the next rung on the ladder: her boss' job—because while Honeywell might be ready for a woman in a high-visibility job, the powerful people who buy and sell companies to and from Honeywell may not be.

"If you talked to my boss, he would agree that in the course of trying to 'back me up'—defending my status to people outside the company—that problem has been an issue for him. It's not so much what he feels, what I feel or what somebody from Honeywell may feel, but it's people at other companies who aren't as enlightened."

Reimer says she's mature enough to accept the situation and find other ways to exert her influence.

"I'm not really impressed with titles, I'm impressed with what I can do to make things happen. And sometimes you can be much more influential letting somebody else have the title and you have the power behind the throne. That's more interesting and more exciting for me."

Reimer says that her talents at collaboration are more important than any particular deal she's done at Honeywell, anyway.

"One of the biggest compliments I've gotten during my career was not how well the deal had been done but how well the members of my team work as a team. And that's important. Because then I help make other people's jobs enjoyable, too."

How to Handle Flak From Your Own Team

In the course of completing a deal, Reimer will frequently require data vital to the negotiation process from different departments within the company.

"I rely on a team of people from various departments to help me do a deal. If there's a tax issue in the deal I go to the tax people, if there's an accounting issue I go to the accounting people, if there are human resources issues I go to them. They don't work for me but they're part of the team."

Unfortunately, many of these individuals act as if they were playing for the opposite team, even though they are Reimer's fellow workers who know exactly what her position is on the organization chart.

As Reimer puts it in her characteristic Midwest understatement: "If you need someone else's expertise and they resent the fact that you have the position that you do, they just don't turn things in on time. These people are just not real excited about doing the extra work necessary to see these transactions get done. Since they don't report to me, I'm not in a position to discipline these people, which is almost a worse situation to be in—I'd have the guts to do that. But you just have to deal with it in some other way."

One approach to the problem is to perform the recalcitrant employee's work yourself. But as Reimer points out, you may learn a lot but you'll work yourself to death in the process.

"The number two approach, which I take generally, is to confront the problem head on by talking to the person. Even if they won't send you memos and they won't respond to questions they can't very well not meet with you.

"And you just go and talk with them, sit with them—go

to their office, don't have them come to yours—and just act like everything's real cool and you have no frustration at all and you're just down there to ask questions. You can never take these situations personally—you always have to be detached. From my perspective that's the only way to address it."

As a lawyer who is trained to "ask the right questions," Reimer's approach is to query the individual in such a way that *he* comes up with the solution: how to get the job done on time.

"I'll ask, 'Who do you have working on the project? What other projects are they working on? Have they been out sick? What is your proposed timetable for completion? What do you see as your problems meeting that timetable? Can we get together in X number of days to discuss it again? If you have any problems I'd like to know about it immediately."

Unfortunately, if options one and two don't work, option number three is to spend money to hire somebody from the outside to do the job the recalcitrant employee should have done in the first place.

"Ten percent of the time I'll just have to say this project isn't going to get done without outside help. And I'll have to get an outside consultant."

As a long distance runner during her rare moments of spare time outside the office, Reimer is accustomed to conserving energy to maintain enough stamina to finish the race. She takes the same approach to solving office conflicts: There's no point in working yourself into a lather over somebody you can't change.

"I think a key to success is never to take any of these conflicts home from the office. I rationalize resistant employee behavior by saying, 'They're behaving this way in their 'business hat' and they probably have a wonderful personality outside the office. It's just that the two of us don't have the same goals, we don't have the same career objectives. And I respect them for what they do but we're not looking for the same thing.' "

"There's No Level Playing Field"

Reimer scoffs at the notion that it's possible to identify companies that are "friendly" to professional women—as if male employees weren't accepted for employment unless they passed a urine test that screened for the right combination of "enlightenment proteins."

"I choke when I see all these articles about the best companies for women to work for."

For one thing, there's no "level playing field" when defining these executive jobs, says Reimer, since whole new categories of management are created within traditional female enclaves to make the numbers look good. "For women, a completely different standard is used to define management than is used for men—it's defined as just about any position in the 'Pink Ps': personnel and public relations."

What's worse, Reimer says, is that women are often promoted not as a reward for their contributions but as a payback for rubber-stamping the ideas of their male superiors. While Reimer says she personally has always been respected at Honeywell for speaking her own mind, she still believes that many women are singled out for advancement because they do precisely the opposite.

"I would rather earn my progress up the ladder rather than be given a position where the job is to agree with somebody that happens to be higher up on it. That's offensive to me."

Long-Term Goals Beyond a Successful M&A Career

Like most of the women profiled in this book and successful women in general, Reimer isn't in the job just for the power and the money.

"It's the constant challenge that comes with the job—It's 'Can I do it?' The mountain's a little bit higher than I thought it would be but can I still climb it? It's the same reason why I run marathons. There's an awful lot of satisfaction that derives from 'the hunt.' A lot of doing things is not what happens when you get there, but it's the process. I really do like the process.

"I'm not interested in easy jobs. That's why when things either come too easily for me or when people put up artificial barriers to make it difficult—such as not respecting you—that's when it's not fun, then it's 'Can-you-outfox-somebody?'

Along with enjoying the thrill of the hunt, she is also interested in leaving her mark somehow in a capacity that's a little more enduring than being a top-notch deal maker.

"My goals aren't necessarily tied into money or anything else but in doing things that make life better.

"To some extent I already do that in the mergers and acquisitions area, because in a way I save people's jobs. If people are in businesses that are not part of our core business it's better for their career if the unit is sold to somebody else who would consider them a mainstream part of their business.

"But there are many days when I'm at work doing these deals selling companies back and forth that I know that I could be doing the world a much greater favor if I were in Appalachia teaching some kid how to read. That's what I call my 'Appalachian days.' I know this sounds 'global' and it sounds trite, but I think you could say that my goal in life is to be in a position to make the world better somehow."

Shirley Prutch
of Martin Marietta:

A PIONEER WHO DID IT HER WAY

Shirley Prutch of Martin Marietta smashed the glass ceiling to top management back when most women were stuck on the ground floor.

She became the first female to be named a vice president of the $5.8 billion corporation in 1979, after having already attained the presidency of Share, an organization of IBM computer users, in 1974. In 1985 she even bridged the career chasm that separates the girls from the boys by securing a "line" vice presidency—running a department that contributes to the bottom line—marketing multimillion dollar computer systems to the government.

How did Prutch get so far against so many odds? Sure, she amassed an impressive track record, tripling sales in a money-losing department and establishing new markets in China, Kuwait and Turkey. But more importantly, she consistently refused to take "No" for an answer when the glass door was slammed in her face. She quit the company in 1968 after being rebuffed for a promotion, she turned down an insultingly inadequate offer to come back in 1970 and threatened to leave once again in mid-1985 to head up a startup software company.

"There were times when I wanted to take the next step in my career and I would talk about it and those in power would say, 'Yeah, yeah, yeah,' " said Prutch in the soft southeastern drawl of her native Maryland. "And nothing would happen. And

53

it was like I had to say to myself, 'Oh, okay, I guess I'll go find a way to accomplish what I want. And it won't be here.' "

Growing up in the 1940s and 1950s, she never dreamed she'd be a standout in the computer field, because the field simply didn't yet exist. As an award-winning scholar and a doted-on only child, Prutch knew she was destined for college and a career, though she thought she'd train to be a teacher, like so many women in that era. It was her parents who convinced her to at least sample other academic pursuits in college besides teaching courses so she'd have a range of career options from which to choose.

"Virtually the only career I had thought about pursuing was teaching because my mother and grandfather had been teachers. My parents asked that I not go to a state teacher's college in case I changed my mind."

After carrying a mind-boggling triple major in mathematics, education, and English at Heidelberg College, Prutch completed her degree at Millersville State Teacher's College in Pennsylvania after all. After graduating in 1957, she taught outside of Philadelphia for five years until she suffered a series of fainting spells in December 1963.

Doctors diagnosed her ailment as anemia and prescribed massive doses of vitamin B-12. When this therapy didn't alleviate her symptoms, she sought a second opinion from a doctor in Denver, where her parents lived, who discovered she had a fibroid tumor of the uterus. Fortunately, the growth proved to be benign. But when she was told after the operation she'd have to be off her feet for at least a year before returning to teaching, Prutch decided to look for a desk job. She applied for a job at Martin Marietta where her father worked "because in Denver there were very few other job alternatives."

"They were looking for something called a programmer. And I said, 'What's a programmer?' And they said, 'You work with computers.' At that time I was so ignorant of the technology, I might as well have asked, 'What's a computer?' "

Prutch signed on as a computer trainee and quickly became immersed in and enthralled with her work. When the Jefferson County school system in Denver tried to lure her back with the post of math supervisor a few months later, Prutch "thought long and hard about it and I said, 'No, I really like what I'm doing.' And I've been in it ever since."

A Pioneer in a New Industry

What stimulated Prutch about the computer field wasn't that the math came easily to her but conversely that the field kept presenting new intellectual challenges as it developed. "I realized at the end of the first year that I was in a field where I was never going to know everything. While initially you'd think you were cock of the walk when you learned something, it would soon dawn on you that you don't know everything, you constantly have to learn how to use this tool. And I was just hooked."

For that very reason, computers appeared to be an ideal industry for women pioneers like Shirley Prutch. "Since computers were a brand new field, nobody really knew anything. If you were willing to work the hours—sometimes 48 in a row—it didn't make any difference if your slacks had a fly in them or not. You just did the work."

Sure enough, Prutch rose quickly within Martin Marietta's fledgling computer department. In her first four years at the company, she moved from trainee programmer to systems analyst to systems programmer. Then in 1968, after she had been appointed "acting" manager when the man with that responsibility left the job, Prutch found out first-hand that if you wanted to *manage* within the computer field, your slacks darned well better have a fly in them.

"My boss called me in and gave me my review, which was outstanding. And he gave me a raise. But he wanted me to know that he just was not going to go to bat for a woman for the manager job; that the company was going to give the title to this other man. But he wanted me to keep doing the work!"

"And I thought, here I am working a heckuva lot harder than a lot of people and making things happen and I should be paid for it *and* have the title.

"I said, 'My God, I expected more than this.'

"And he replied, 'But Shirley, you're single. You're young.'

"I protested, 'But I'm working my butt off.' "

Prutch says that her boss' rationale for passing her over for the promotion was that "since I could afford to buy a Buick Skylark convertible I should be able to manage on my current salary. And, of course, I was a single person and the man they wanted to give the job to had just had his third child. While I don't make excuses for my boss, I think his views reflected the thinking of that period."

While Prutch could understand the rationale for the man's decision, that didn't mean she was going to accept it.

"I went home and told my mom and dad, 'They're giving the job to so-and-so and not me. So I'm going to look for another job.' And they said, 'Good for you.' "

Prutch is grateful to have basked in her parents' pride throughout her career. "I have always known my parents were behind me. They have truly provided a support system."

Luckily, Prutch could not only rely on her parent's support but the fact that economics were in her favor. In 1968 there was a mounting demand within the industry for technical people who knew anything about the young computer field and only a small supply of those were highly skilled people. She had already been hounded by headhunters and had fended them off, but now that the manager title was denied her she was receptive to their calls. "I had some headhunters call about a job opportunity that same afternoon or the next day and I said, 'Yeah, I'd be interested.' "

She was offered a challenging opportunity to start a computer department from scratch for King Resources, a new oil and gas exploration company in Denver. This time, nobody begrudged her a title: Director of Computer Resources.

Prutch's bosses back at Martin Marietta were flabbergasted when she served notice. "When I went in and gave them two weeks notice it was, 'Well, you can't.' And I said, 'Well, I am.' "

When the impact of her departure finally sunk in two weeks after she left, one of her old bosses tried to lure her back, but to no avail. "He came down to my new employer and took me to lunch and he said 'Shirley, I didn't know you were leaving. My God, please come back.' I said, 'Thank you very much but I like what I'm doing.'

"And I kept in touch with them. I didn't burn any bridges. This whole thing happened to me before the era when the accepted thing would be to file a lawsuit."

Actually, the "accepted thing" in that era would have been for a young women to subscribe to her boss' logic and stay at Martin Marietta despite the affront, accepting the notion that male heads of households are the ones who get promoted, whereas single women—who are destined to become housewives anyway and therefore constitute poor personnel "investments"—are not.

In retrospect, Prutch believes that the reason she didn't conform to that belief structure was that she was a product of an unusual extended family whose members expected women to follow their own instincts and not follow convention.

"My grandmother was a very different woman, very much ahead of her time. She was much younger than my grandfather when they got married and while he wanted to settle down, she still wanted to be 'at the dances.' After her daughter, my mother, was born, my grandmother walked out on my grandfather and was traveling from here to there sowing her wild oats, I guess you'd say. She ultimately married another man. So my mother wound up being raised by her mother's sister-in-law: my grandfather's sister."

In another household, even today, Prutch's grandmother would most certainly have been vilified by her family members as a 'loose woman' and, worse, one who reneged on her primary responsibility as a mother. But Prutch's mother, father, and grandfather not only continued to speak well of her but welcomed her back into the fold when she decided to rejoin them.

Not only were people with unconventional lifestyles accepted by Prutch's family, but those with opposing viewpoints as well.

"For one thing, my parents never talked down to me. A conversation in our house wasn't a 'What-did-you-do-in-school?', pat-on-the-head type of thing, but a discussion about something I was studying. I always thought it odd when I'd be at a friend's for dinner and hear the parents talk down to the kids.

"For another, we didn't make 'small talk' around the dinner table, it was more often a debate about something that was happening in the world between my grandfather, who believed one way and my mother, who believed another and my father, who had a third opinion. Everybody had something to say and everybody's opinion was heard."

Timing Isn't Everything: A Job Offer She Had to Refuse

Prutch's decision not to burn her career bridges back to Martin Marietta paid off, although not right away. Less than two years after she joined King Resources, the company filed for bank-ruptcy. While its management was perfectly willing to keep her on in a different area of the company, Prutch said no. "They got rid of the computer and I didn't want to work for a company without a computer."

Just as she was about to give notice at King Resources, the management at Martin Marietta told her they were starting a new computer subsidiary, Data Systems, in Towson, Md. and she was asked if she would consider coming back. The timing proved to be right, but that was about all.

Prutch was flown back to Baltimore and was interviewed by a man who had been her boss' boss six years before when she joined the company. Her responsibilities in the start-up sounded challenging. "He told me about what they were going to do and I was very excited."

But when another manager started hemming and hawing about her position in this start-up, her excitement turned to annoyance: it was "*deja vu* all over again."

"He started saying things like, 'We'll have to be careful what your title is when we bring you back because So-and-so who taught your training class is only a such-and-such.' And: 'Oh, Shirley, you're making a lot of money at King Resources and if you had stayed at Martin Marietta you'd only be making this amount.' " As though that were supposed to make her accept less salary!

Adding insult to injury, since the personnel department wasn't used to dealing with female executives, the officials talked to her about the only "female" issue they knew how to discuss—babies. "They talked to me about pregnancy benefits! I wasn't even married!," says Prutch in disgust. "So I sat there and listened to this. Then they took me out to the airport and made the offer."

Never one to react in anger, Prutch's response was, "I'll get back to you."

During the three-hour plane ride back to Denver, however, the more she turned over in her mind what transpired in the interview, the madder she got.

"I thought to myself, 'I can't go back into this situation—what do you mean not tell people what my title is! Because it's higher than somebody else! That's craziness.' "

Sam, her husband, whom she had met at King Resources and married four years later, met her at the plane.

And he asked, 'How's your trip? Did you get the job offer?'

"I said, 'Yeah, I got it. But Sam, you'll never believe this.' And he said, 'What?'

"I told him, 'First of all they talked to me about pregnancy benefits. Then they told me I couldn't be a director because after all, this guy had that title and he taught my training class.'

"Sam said, 'What does that have to do with anything?' And I said, 'That's what I say.' "

It was clear that Martin Marietta was once again trying to tap Prutch's talents without affording her any power. It was clearly an offer she had to refuse.

"In my mind they had ruined it. And my mindset was, why should I go back into that? At least at King Resources management's approach was: 'Here's your title, it's director of regional technology, this is what we want you to do. And here's the salary.' They didn't pussy foot around."

Prutch instead went to work for a computer sharing company service called Rio Grande Industries, owned by Denver, Western and Rio Grande Railroad. Her title: Vice-President of Operations. But getting that title was no piece of cake.

"I was told, 'You can't have a woman be a Vice-President.'

"And I looked at the man who was President of the railroad and asked, 'Mr. So-and-so, why not?'

"He answered, 'Well, hell I don't know.'

"I said, 'What are the qualifications for the job, does it start with *male*?'

"He said, 'No Shirley, you're absolutely right, it doesn't.'

"I told him, 'Well, then, let's talk about what I'm supposed to do.' And we ultimately got to be very good friends."

Prutch says her guiding philosophy in deciding to stand up for her rights in the workplace has been logic, not ideology. She's always distanced herself from feminist doctrine on workplace issues. She loathes quotas as a mechanism for enforcing equal rights. She resisted pantsuits when they became trendy in the 1970s because she thought they distracted attention to one's wardrobe and away from her ideas. She never took offense when her male colleagues would joke about "kissing a Vice President" once she attained that status because she assumed they did so out of sheer awkwardness.

But just try to tell her that a woman can't do a certain job. Or that maybe she can do it, but she shouldn't get the same money or status as a man in the same job. And watch the sparks fly.

"I guess when people said no, a woman can't do something,

I just react and say, 'Why?' Throughout my career, if there were a logical reason that a woman couldn't do a certain job, that would be one thing. But if it was a stupid reason, and none of the qualifications made any difference, my reaction was, well, why *can't* I do that? And, what do you mean 'They won't talk to a woman?' The issue isn't whether you're a woman or a man it's what qualities of leadership are you giving to this group?"

Prutch believes she was able to force the issue of fairness on her employers because she was in the right industry at the right time—and she had the right mind.

"I never had a feeling that any of my employers hired me as a way to fill a quota, it was because of what I could offer to the job. Sometimes that meant knowledge of how computers and systems worked and later on during my career it meant using computers to get things done and then finally it manifested itself as managing the people to get the job done."

Prutch faced another career juncture two years after she joined Rio Grande Industries when its management decided to sell the company, a week after she and Sam were married and began moving into their new home. Once again, Martin Marietta came courting. And this time they had done their homework.

"The same VP that had taken me to lunch after I had quit the first time came to me and said, 'We'd like you to come back as Director of Regional Technology and here's your office—he had already put my name on the door—and here's your offer letter.'

"I looked at the letter and I said, 'I can't believe this.'

"And he said, 'Come on, you don't want to stay where you are. We're getting a data systems company started and we need you and we want you. And you and I are going to go drink martinis until you accept. And besides, I've already called Sam—they'd been trying to hire him also—and told him that I was going to make you the offer and I promised I would stop bothering him once I get you.' "

Looking back at her career, Prutch is certain that if she hadn't done it "her way," leaving Martin Marietta and coming back on her own terms, she never would have made it to Vice President, but would have been named to a token supervisory position.

"Maybe I'm Monday-morning-quarterbacking, but I think If I'd stayed at Martin Marietta instead of leaving those times I did, the farthest I would have gone within the company would have been supervisor or a Director of Technology because at a certain point they would have felt pressure to move some women into jobs such as these. But I'd never be in a management position."

You Can Get There From Here: From Technician to Manager

By the mid-1970s, Prutch had won recognition throughout the computer industry not only for her technical expertise but her management skills as well.

Most of her stature outside of the company came from her involvement in Share, an organization of companies using IBM® mainframes who would compare notes on different ways to use software. While she didn't join Share in order to *network* (meet others in her field who could help her advance), it seemed to turn out that way. And networking is something every woman can do to advance her career. Even more impressive than the influence her affiliation with Share had on her career at Martin Marietta however, was the impact she had on it: the organization was so smitten with her take-no-prisoners management style that she walked into her first meeting in 1974 a mere member and walked out an officer.

Prutch had been asked to serve on a Share committee that coordinated an upcoming meeting in Denver, a massive undertaking, since it required scheduling 25 concurrent meetings in four time slots during the day and two time slots in the evening. After she asked a few questions, it soon became evident that if she didn't take charge of this committee the meeting would literally become a nonevent, so botched were all the arrangements.

"They had a deadline by which all the meeting rooms and the number of attendees had to be relayed to the hotels—and probably three-fourths of the information wasn't in. Nobody took these kind of deadlines seriously."

Prutch attributes the state of disarray to nothing more profound than garden-variety computer nerdiness, the inability of techies to break away from their number-crunching and stoop to the task of sorting out the dull, mundane details of administration. Says Prutch with a chuckle: "You know how these guys are: 'You mean I have to fill out a time card? What for?' "

But Prutch wasn't only a technician, she was a manager. So, commando-style, she deployed her committee members to conduct a massive 11th hour phoneathon to salvage the event and circulate a program to the hundreds of participants. Mission accomplished, she marched up to Share's management and gave them a dressing-down.

"In this whole hullabaloo, I kind of took the Share hierarchy to task. I told them, 'You guys don't know what you're doing. You don't run an organization this way. You've got to be able to show a corporation like IBM that you can behave like managers, not like techies!' "

The Share management was so impressed with Prutch's forthrightness, they offered her a promotion on the spot.

"At that very meeting, the officers of Share were incorporating the organization and the duties of treasurer and secretary were being split up. So they offered me the treasurer job. I guess the President figured that if I were given all these responsibilities he could make sure I'd become an active member of Share rather than just a meeting attendee."

Having already had a taste of the organization's mismanagement, Prutch was not one to take this so-called promotion at face value. "I found out how much money I was taking over and I said, 'Have you audited the account? Because I'm not going to take it over until it's audited.' She also saw to it that the money was somewhere making some money, not languishing in a mattress. "They had all sorts of money—tens of thousands of dollars—sitting in a checking account and not even gaining interest. I said, 'Why don't we put it into CDs or Treasury notes, this is crazy!'

"Their approach to running the organization was, 'Well, this is something we've always done.' My attitude is that if you're going to do something you'd better by God do it the best way you can or don't do it at all. So suddenly I got some prominence, people listened to me."

Did her membership in Share influence her career climb at Martin Marietta? Prutch doesn't know for sure. "I think my promotions came primarily because management saw that I could pick the right staff, manage people, delegate assignments, and fix mistakes quickly. But it certainly doesn't hurt your career if your boss' boss is at a big meeting with somebody you've worked with at Share and that somebody talks to your big boss and says, "I worked with Shirley Prutch on such-and-such a project and, my, wasn't she great!"

Prutch has watched this dynamic at work in some of her other "extracurricular" activities outside of her job. "When I did some work for the National Academy of Sciences the chairman of my committee was at a dinner with Norm Augustine, now chairman of Martin Marietta. The man said to Norm, "Would you happen to know Shirley Prutch?" Norm said, "Of course." This man said, "Well, I've got to tell you if I could hire Shirley I would love to."

Whether or not her activity in Share helped her internal progress at Martin Marietta, it clearly made her visible with America's computer community.

"In the mid-1970s the President of IBM's World Trade division asked me to speak to the presidents of the various IBM divisions at a meeting in Paris about the idea that women could be more than technologists. I was president of Share at the time and this man had been impressed with what I had accomplished. He told me, 'Just talk openly to them about being a woman manager, tell them how it's different.' "

But since Prutch doesn't believe in the doctrine of separate-but-equal in the workplace, she talked to them instead about what makes a good manager. But not before breaking the ice with a joke. "The only difference I could think of to talk about was, 'When I look around a room at all of you men, I know that when we take a break everyone else will be able to find the men's room but I've got to figure out where the ladies' room is on my own. And sometimes I have to find the key.' "

While the men who worked in management information systems may have started getting used to seeing a woman among their management ranks during the early 1970s, the notion still appeared to produce cognitive dissonance among their wives.

That same year Prutch represented the U.S. at a meeting of the International Federation of Information Processing, whose function was to disseminate the importance of data processing worldwide. Her husband, Sam, accompanied her to the meeting's idyllic location on the island of Corsica. Indeed Sam accompanied her frequently on out of town trips.

According to the agenda, the meeting participants would get together to discuss business in the morning, sightsee in the afternoons, and meet again in the evening. The spouses would be taken on their own sightseeing trips while the meetings were going on.

Shirley and Sam were enjoying themselves immensely, although they were baffled by an unsettling coolness emanating from the participants' wives. As she put it: "The wives of the other members of the group were not very nice or very cordial to Sam, which I couldn't understand."

Sam found out why during the second day of the conference, while he was standing waiting for the sightseeing bus.

"As Sam was standing there putting on his name tag that said 'spouse,' one of the wives looked at him and said, 'Excuse me, is your *wife* the delegate?' And he said, 'Yes, she is.'

"The women all started to talk to each other and it turned out, to make a long story short, they had thought that Sam was the delegate, not me, and he had been skipping out on the meetings and sending me instead to stand in for him while he went out and had a good time.

"Well, he thought this was incredibly funny. He got on the bus and he absolutely captivated this group with the real story. The ones who could speak English would translate the story for the ones whose English wasn't so good and everybody started to laugh. And he totally charmed them."

Not only was Sam Prutch proud of the international status that his wife had attained, he gave her a dressing down during an occasion on that very same trip when she tried to downplay it.

"As we were flying back from Corsica and circling over New York making small talk to the other passengers, this man next to me asked where I had been. I told him Corsica and he said, 'On business?' and I said yes.

"And he said, 'Wow, isn't it nice that your husband took you along!' I answered, 'Yes, it's great.'

"And Sam leaned over to the guy and said, 'I don't mean to embarrass you but my wife took *me* along.'

"I looked at Sam and I told him, 'You didn't need to say that,' and he said, 'Shirley! You know that's not right!'

The Benefits of a Supportive Husband

Prutch attributes a good measure of her career success to her husband, Sam, a fellow computer manager she met at King

Resources who assumed her post when she left to go to Rio Grande Industries.

Sam Prutch didn't just adopt the traditional spousal role of morale booster and sounding board but agreed to let her career take precedence. He assumed the 'trailing spouse' role when her promotions took her to different cities, put up with living apart for a year when he wasn't able to find a job near hers—essentially made a psychological leap to second fiddle that few spouses of professional women are able to make even today.

"My husband, if he had chosen, could have gone as far as I did in his career—if not further—because whatever he has chosen to do, he has done to perfection," says Prutch. "But instead he took his free time and vacations to go with me to meetings to be supportive; he was definitely there for me." Rather than seeing this role as one of sacrifice, "he says he considers himself lucky because he got to travel to interesting places."

How do we account for Sam's enlightened outlook? Did he, like his wife, have an unusual "equal opportunity" upbringing? Prutch can barely stifle a snicker at this suggestion. "You don't mind if I laugh, do you? No, on the contrary, later on in my career when we went to Pueblo, Colorado to tell his dad and mother about the fact we'd be moving from Denver to Washington because of a promotion I just got, their reaction was, 'You're doing WHAT? For *her* job?' And Sam's boyhood friends, two of whom still visit us, still don't understand my career, although we're still very good friends."

Women executives like Prutch not only have to get used to doing without respect and admiration from their extended families for their career accomplishments, but frequently find themselves the "odd woman out" at office parties. During these social gatherings the sexes usually part like the Red Sea, with the women talking 'kuchen and kinder' in the kitchen and the guys sharing sports scores or shop talk in the living room.

"Many times when we'd be in parties, especially in Washington, I'd just end up with the men talking business, rather than with the women talking about cookies and the schools and so forth. Sure, I enjoy cooking and I can talk about that for a little while. But when they started talking about soap operas I'd excuse myself and go talk business with the guys."

"Lady Boss" Ahead of Her Time

While Prutch readily acknowledges that it hasn't been easy convincing management that she wanted and deserved the next
rung up the ladder as much as the "next guy" during the course
of her career, she maintains that even in the unenlightened
1970s it wasn't as difficult being taken seriously as a woman
as one might have expected.

"I suppose when I look back at it, I should have been very
upset by various setbacks—because of all the publicity about
sex discrimination, because of the woman's movement, and the
laws that have been passed to promote equal opportunity. And
sometimes I ask myself, 'Why wasn't I angry that the people I
worked with didn't take me for what I was—that I always had
to prove myself?'

"And maybe I wasn't angry because I also enjoyed distinct
benefits from being 'the only woman.' Because everybody paid
attention to me. As the only woman at senior management
meetings everybody would want me to sit at their table. And
it's not because you're beautiful or you're great, it's because
you're the only woman there.

"When it came to proving yourself on the job, you only had
to do something right once because it was such a shock to some
of these people that you did it right. To tell the truth, the only
thing you had to worry about was that you didn't get such a
big head."

If anything, Prutch says that during the 1970s the legitimacy of her management status was threatened less by the
fact that women were a rarity than by the growing practice
among employers to use a quota system; i.e., hire a certain
percentage of women for selected jobs—that occasionally created the impression that she was a pawn in "the numbers
game."

"There would be times when I would walk into a new job
environment and there would be people who seemed to be
thinking, "Ugh, here's another 'number,' and not somebody
who legitimately deserved the job."

Not surprisingly, during that same period Prutch was also
besieged by phone calls from companies seemingly eager to

expand those numbers and "show her off," rather than offer jobs with substance.

"I would get a lot of job offers during that period, just out of the blue. But when the people with the jobs would start to talk to me, it would be in terms of "corner offices," the perks, never anything about what the job was going to be. And that to me is an absolutely dead giveaway that it's a token job."

Despite the absence of female colleagues with which to commiserate about the day-to-day frustrations of managing people, Prutch says that she never had problems having heart-to-heart talks about these concerns with her male colleagues.

"I've always felt that I've had a high level of camaraderie with men," which Prutch attributes to the fact that growing up she had plenty of "boy friends," not just "boyfriends." "I always had lots of boys hanging around the house who were friends and not dates. When I was in high school there was a male friend who would come over and visit who virtually lived at our house, he probably ate more meals at our house than at his."

Dealing with Co-workers Who Suspect Your Authority

Of course, Prutch did have to confront male colleagues who weren't used to seeing women as equals during the course of her career. When she was appointed director of the Denver computing center in 1978, "I had to deal with a group of hard-nosed engineers in the aerospace group who were definitely not used to seeing a woman at a staff meeting."

Nor was it only the engineers, but the vice-president in charge of engineering for the Titan missile who at one point challenged Prutch's authority by claiming her staff was incompetent.

"He was saying that our computer room people were not doing their job and that they were 'dropping their decks of cards.' Except that we hadn't used computer cards for years. Basically, he was trying to use my staff and their services as scapegoats for his people not getting their work done.

"I said, 'Chuck, I don't know what you're talking about.

But if you're talking about cards, we haven't used cards for 10 years.' I told him he was supposed to look at the performance that we had been providing, that that's what I was there to talk to him about.

"So I think the fact that I could figure out what was behind all of this enabled me to call his bluff. To this day, he's a good friend. He just wasn't used to dealing with a woman."

A year later when Prutch was promoted to director of the Orlando aerospace account, a year-long assignment, Sam was offered a job in the aerospace division of the business but he turned it down because the couple maintains a strict policy against working for the same company, even if they're in different ends of the business. Prutch says they made the rule because they don't want their loyalty to each other to sabotage their objectivity in dealing with other co-workers.

"For example, I could come home from work one day and let off steam about somebody at work and the next day I may come home and think this person is an absolute angel. But meanwhile, out of loyalty to me, my husband might still be angry at this person."

Sam was unable to find a job with any challenge in Orlando so he wound up staying in Denver for that year and they endured a commuter marriage. "My husband and I figured we could stick out the long distance bit because it would only be a short period of time before I was up for another promotion and I'd be coming back to Denver."

In Orlando, Prutch once again had to confront hostility—expressed in the form of anxiety—from male subordinates. "My first meeting was with a group of men who had never ever had a woman in their midst, much less as their boss, and you could have almost cut the tension with a knife. They asked me things like, 'How can we hold a meeting without using any four-letter words?' 'Are we supposed to hold doors open for you?' And 'How should we introduce you to our customers?' "

Her approach this time was to address these fears indirectly by showing them how her female status could be used to the group's advantage in certain work situations. This diplomatic approach made enough of an impression that one of the men who attended the first staff meeting brought the incident up in a conversation on the occasion of her retirement in August 1990, 11 years later.

"He told me, 'Shirley, I can remember you said to us, 'Just

remember, sometimes my being a woman can get you in places where you guys otherwise couldn't go, so don't feel bad about using me in that role.' What I meant by that is that there were many times that because I was a woman I could approach a secretary who had absolute control over access to the president's office and be able to appeal to her to get through to him. I would tell her who I was, why I wanted to get in and the minute she heard whatever my title was at the time, her reaction would be, 'Oh my God, here's a woman!' and she would help me."

Handling Recalcitrant Subordinates

Prutch says she's never had to deal with subordinates who didn't perform up to speed because they didn't respect her authority as a female boss. On the other hand, she felt no qualms about confronting "bad actors" who were simply unproductive—unlike some women who have a tough time viewing themselves as authority figures.

"I've never had any problem dealing with people working for me who start to show an attitude problem—to sulk or make snide remarks. When somebody does that, I guess my adrenalin starts to boil and my self-confidence emerges. When I'm confronted with that attitude, I've simply closed my office door and had a 'Come to Jesus' with the guy.

"I've told the person, 'We're not going to put up with this. This is not the way I do business. If you've got a problem, you best tell me what it is. If you've got something on your mind, you better get that fixed. And if you need a couple of days off to do it, you've got it. But if you don't need a couple of days off, then when you walk in here tomorrow morning you better be a different man or I want your resignation.' "

Prutch makes a distinction, however, between subordinates with a chip on their shoulder and those who, try as they might, are simply unable to perform because of some flaw in her management style.

"I have absolutely worried about a person who is not showing their full potential, because I'm not getting through to the guy because I'm a woman. I'd ask myself, What am I doing that is bothering him? That would worry me. But when somebody reaches the point of making snide remarks and not doing their work, there's no middle ground."

Socializing With the Guys

Life for women executives can be lonely at the top, especially when it comes time for lunch. The male corporate culture ostensibly dictates that it's not proper for women to ask male colleagues to join them "because they might take it the wrong way" or the woman might inhibit their ability to engage in such lunchtime male-bonding rituals as debating which century the Chicago Cubs will win the World Series.

Prutch says that women have to stop being wallflowers and start being the aggressors, a role they don't have a lot of experience playing.

"I have observed women who are about to become peers with the men and have to leave the comfort of having women around them, and they seem to feel threatened by that experience."

She relates the example of a woman on the cusp of executivehood, tray in hand, who agonizes over where to sit in the company cafeteria. "Let's say you have a choice of sitting at two tables. At the first table are the women you've worked with before and maybe some secretaries. And at the other table are men who had been a level higher than you who are now your peers. The easy, comfortable thing is to sit with the women—and most women do it.

"And my approach is, you suck in your gut and you smile at the women and say 'Hello,' and then you turn to the men and say, 'May I join you?' "

Nor should women "wait to be asked" when it comes for after-hours socializing, says Prutch.

"When you're traveling with a group and you're all out together and somebody says, 'Hey, let's go get a drink,' if that individual just looks at the guys, you say, 'Any problem if I join you?' They usually don't have enough sense to say no."

Mentors Should Be Teachers and Not String-Pullers

As is the case for most of the women profiled in this book, Prutch believes that it's important to look to a mentor for advice on succeeding in management. But she draws a distinct Maginot line between relying on an experienced executive to teach you the ropes and one who pulls strings for you, in much the same way she has distanced herself from feminist workplace doctrine on such issues as hiring by quotas. "When I read anything on mentors they're always described as individuals who make sure that if there is a choice between two people for a certain job that you're the one who gets chosen. Well, if that's what it takes for a woman to succeed, I think our whole system has gone to pot. Your success has got to be based on whether you can do the job and what you have done to show that you can.

"My personal definition of mentors are the people, men or women, who gave me a one-shot piece of advice or a lot of good advice, who helped me think things through or made me reconsider my own ideas."

For example, Prutch said she would consider as mentor a fellow member of Share who didn't work for Martin Marietta, who among other things helped her realize that she didn't need to prove herself as a "techie" to be a good manager.

"He told me, 'You know, you're an excellent technician, you're one of the best technical people I've ever met, but you can't be both a manager and a techie. In our field you can't keep up with the bits, the bytes and all of the technical stuff and be a good manager because there's not enough time. You don't have to be able to DO something that you manage, you only have to be smart enough to *understand* it. So he convinced me I didn't need to go to the internal computer classes anymore."

Banging the Glass Ceiling

At the end of 1979, Prutch was transferred back to Washington as Vice President of Martin Marietta's account division. Sam found a job with the company that ran the computing center for the Executive Office of the President.

But it wasn't easy for her husband to convince prospective employers about his long-term commitments to the Washington area. Prutch says, "He found out firsthand what "trailing wives" have to endure when their husbands are transferred and they go job hunting. When he'd apply for a job, people would ask him why he had moved here. He'd say, 'My wife works for Martin Marietta and she was promoted.' And they'd reply, 'Why should we give you a job? What if your wife moves again?' He is convinced that's what women put up with when their husbands are transferred."

As vice-president and general manager of the company's accounts division, Prutch was responsible for all of the data processing within Martin Marietta. Not only had she become the company's first female Vice President, but joined only a handful of women in the nation who had attained that level. That distinction produced a bit of confusion and pride among her colleagues.

"When I was made a vice-president at Martin Marietta the standard joke by these guys was, 'Gee, I've never kissed a vice-president before.'

"Some women would ask me, 'That's terrible, why do you put up with it?' Why? I put up with it because the guys weren't doing it out of rudeness. In their own way they were expressing praise, it was pride. So I didn't take it as a put-down."

While Prutch never objected to good-natured joking about her position, she always took her job responsibilities and her career challenges seriously. And she wasn't satisfied with simply having the vice-president's title. She wanted to jump over the chasm that seemingly separates the men from the boys— or more accurately: the girls from the boys—opportunities to work in a line capacity, helping the company make money.

"I wanted to do more than the information systems side of Martin Marietta, the internal work, I wanted to see if I could sell."

So in 1985 she went to the top brass and put in a bid for the job running the company's systems integration division, which designs, integrates and operates large-scale computer systems for federal government agencies. And, as usual, her career aspirations were a step ahead of her superiors. Her request was turned down.

"They told me, 'We can't afford to have you leave. Nobody else can do the job you're doing.'

"And I answered, 'That's baloney. I'm going to go look for a job elsewhere.'

"They told me, 'Don't be silly.' And they all thought, 'She won't do this.' "

Prutch didn't have to look hard for new career opportunities. As was the case 20 years earlier when the computer industry was in its infancy, opportunities sought her, this time because of her national reputation as a manager. She got a call from a headhunter, most likely tipped off by her mentor in Share, who was prospecting for someone to run a start-up software company.

Prutch followed up and was offered the job. But saying yes was easier than saying goodbye to Martin Marietta, since once again her impending absence made management's heart grow fonder. When she gave notice, "The full court press came from Martin Marietta to get me to change my mind. "I told them 'I'm sorry, but I've given my word, I can't back down.' "

At that point management got down on bended knee. They offered her the job at Martin Marietta she asked for in the first place. They threw in a few sweeteners to seal the deal: a raise and a car.

Then when all the perks didn't succeed in tipping the balance, pressure was exerted. While Prutch was still agonizing over which offer to accept, "The president came down and sat in my office and told me, 'I don't know what your problem is. A lot of people go through what you're going through. If you want, I'll get on the phone and call the man for you and tell him you're not coming.' He was putting me right on the spot. He knew exactly how to.

"I said, 'If anyone is going to call him, I'll call him.'

"And he said, 'Do you want me to tell you what to say?' And I said no.

"So I called the man who was running the company and when I opened with, 'Dick, this is Shirley Prutch,' before I could get another word out he said, 'Oh, Shirley, you're not coming.' "

Prutch's heart leapt to her throat. "I asked him, 'How do you know?' Naturally, I thought the president had already told him and I said to myself: I'm going to kill him.

"But he hadn't been tipped off, he just had a sixth sense why I was calling. 'Shirley,' he told me, 'I've never thought from the beginning that 'Martin' would let you get out of there. We knew it was a long shot when we took the chance to try and get you.' "

While Prutch was flattered to have been considered for the job, she felt that she violated her personal standards of integrity by going back on her word and reneging. "That man is still a friend today. But I don't think it's one of the very best parts of my life. To this day I don't feel that's one of my high points. Because I had said, 'Yes, I will come.' And I didn't."

Her Future: A Surprise Ending

Probably more than any other woman profiled in this book, Shirley Prutch would have had an excellent shot at the CEO's job had she chosen to pursue that prize. But Prutch doesn't aspire to power for its own sake. So in August of 1990 she handed in her resignation.

But this time it wasn't to look for greener pastures and greater challenges but to take a breather. Prutch said that after working like mad together for 30 years, she and her husband craved precious time to relax together.

"During most of my career, twelve-hour days were the norm, not counting take-home work. Sam and I thought we needed the time together. We do like each other's company. So we're going to see if we like it all of the time."

Prutch probably won't relax too long because she's already knee-deep in a second career: teaching illiterate adults to read—an extension of the teaching career that was cut short by illness in 1963.

"This sounds very hokey, but I like to 'give something back' and one of the things I always wanted to do is teach adults how to read. I just can't think of a situation more humiliating than to be an otherwise perfectly able adult who is not able to read. Because I love to read, reading to me is a Godsend. Having traveled in other countries, I've experienced what it's like to be unable to decipher the signs and menus. That's exactly what these illiterate adults are experiencing—except it's with the language they grew up with!"

With her characteristic modesty, Prutch recoils at any attempts to characterize her as a pioneer among women in management. "I don't consider myself someone special, I just did what needed to be done. And when I felt that I was doing my job to the best of my abilities and I was not allowed to progress I just looked for another place to progress."

Looking back at the more than two decades she dedicated to Martin Marietta, Prutch says while she had to confront, "But Shirley, you can't" far too often in her career, even those individuals who didn't take her seriously in the beginning wound up being wowed by her accomplishments.

On the occasion of a going-away party held for her in 1979 when she was leaving Orlando for Washington, D.C., "I got a note from the gentleman who told me in 1968 that he wasn't going to give me the management job. He wrote that he always joked that he gave me the 'encouragement'—the wrong way— but the encouragement to succeed. And when I came back to Martin Marietta and he wound up working for me instead of the other way around, I couldn't have had a person that was prouder of me. He was truly proud."

The former president of the company, whom Prutch counts among her close friends, was also one of her well-wishers on her "retirement," in his own way.

"He told me, 'You accomplished so many things over the years that we never thought were possible.'

"And I said, 'Tom, if you didn't think it was possible, why the hell did you send me to do them?'

"He answered, 'Shirl, That's a goddam good question!'"

The more pointed rejoinder might have been, "If I was so terrific, why the hell did I have to fight for every goddam promotion?"

But, then again, that wouldn't have been Shirley Prutch's style.

chapter 6

Nancy Faunce
of Eastman Kodak:

BREAKING GROUND IN A MALE-DOMINATED FIELD

Nobody could argue that Nancy Faunce rode the fast track during her first 13 years in the computer field by simply being in the right place at the right time. She had to prove herself to a skeptical boss, win the respect of snickering colleagues, and dazzle hard-drinking, ink-under-the-fingernails customers before she could establish a track record.

By 1988, Nancy Faunce counted herself among an elite corps of a dozen top woman executives at Eastman Kodak Company. She headed up one of the company's fastest growing units, Kodak Legal Systems, which she built virtually from scratch while KLS was still part of Atex, Inc., a computer-aided publishing company that Kodak acquired in 1981. She was a sought-after speaker, before business and academic groups on the subject of "intrapreneurship," the building of startups within large corporations. In 1990, she was nominated for *Inc.* magazine's Entrepreneur of the Year.

And though Kodak has reversed the picture on Nancy Faunce as of this writing by closing down Kodak Legal Systems, Faunce's story can still tell us much about banging the glass ceiling.

Climbing the Ladder From the First Rung

Armed with a degree in economics from Wellesley College, Faunce entered the computer field in 1978 as a sales trainee for a

Billerica, Massachusetts company called Atex that produced newspaper computer systems.

"Going to a small company such as Atex rather than a large company like IBM was a wise choice because it gave me exposure to the chief executive and the key players in the company at an early point in my career. My role models were the president and the vice-president of human resources, who were very committed to the development of their employees, who were fanatical about the learning process. The president would collar you in a hallway conversation and he'd challenge you to think of new ways of solving problems. It was an environment that conveyed the message, 'There aren't any limits here except for those that you set yourself.' "

The vice president believed that she should learn the business from the ground up and told the company's national sales director to develop her. Unfortunately, far from sharing the vice-president's lofty view of women, her boss put her in a Catch 22 box: refusing to let her sell because she had no experience, and refusing to give her any experience.

"He pointed out that the rest of the sales force had at least a dozen years of experience under their belts and I had none. Of course, if I had been a guy, he would have treated me as somebody coming up through the ranks and trained me."

Faunce begged her boss to give her a shot at pounding the pavement but he told her to cool her heels in the office, writing the description of the job she'd like to do, if she ever got a chance.

"When you don't want to let somebody work, you tell them to write their own job description. I went through that drill by writing six pages of job description and leaving six pages blank. My boss would say, 'What are these blank pages for?' and I'd answer, 'That's *your* half.' I felt like I was doing work that he should have been doing."

After performing that exercise in futility for two weeks, Faunce decided it was time to shop for a new employer. No sooner had she started polishing up her resume when "the Senior Vice President got wind of it somehow and I got taken to lunch."

"He asks me, 'So how many resumes do you have out on the street? What's going on?' "

"I told him, 'Here you put me in sales but my boss is jerking me around and not letting me work. And I'm not going to sit around and wait and play games.' "

The Vice President evidently 'had a chat' with Faunce's boss and she was subsequently allowed to make sales calls. The end of the story is that at the end of the year she wound up on top of the heap as the number one salesperson. "And then following that I was either number one or number two for the entire time I was in sales."

Did her boss ever apologize for attempting to waylay her career? On the contrary, he tried to take credit for it.

"What's ironic is that this same guy thinks he was my biggest mentor. When my career started taking off, he acted like a proud papa. Isn't it funny how history gets reinterpreted?"

Winning Respect from Colleagues

Along with demonstrating to her superiors that she could cut it in sales, Faunce also had to endure the psychological equivalent of having her pigtail dunked in the inkwell.

"When I lost my first couple of sales, my 'supportive associates' would say, 'Do you think you're losing them because you're a woman?' I answered, 'I don't know, I can't exactly do the comparison because I can't become a man.'

"Then they'd put you through this wonderful initiation rite called, 'Let's see if we can make her cry.' They'd tease me about being 'a women's libber,' and that kind of stuff."

She also had to endure snide remarks from jealous employees who hinted that her success was due to getting a leg up from her friends in high places.

"Soon after I started at Atex, a guy who was turned down when he asked to move into sales came into my office to complain about how unfair it was that I was being given the opportunity and not himself—just because I had gone to Wellesley and he had only graduated from such-and-such a university. He went on to ask me why I thought I was good enough to be in sales and who in the company did I know to get this job, etcetera, etcetera."

Faunce believes that when the going gets tough, humor is a great equalizer and so she'd tolerate such silliness with amused restraint. "For example, let's say I'm in a restaurant with the other salesmen and when a woman would pass by the table they'd make some comment about some part of her anatomy. So when a man passed I'd comment on some parts of *his* anatomy. If I'm lucky, I'd make them blush.

"If I knew they were just trying to bait me I'd ignore them. If it got too obnoxious I'd tell them what I thought of them. But I knew they were doing it as much to provoke a reaction as anything else."

Faunce believes that if you assume that men sometimes behave immaturely around women out of sheer awkwardness and not hostility, you'll put yourself in a better mental state to achieve parity. You may get groove marks on your tongue from biting it so hard but you'll end up the victor.

"I made the assumption that nobody was trying to 'get me,' it was just that as a woman I was a novelty and they didn't know how to deal with me. My attitude was that they needed to be educated and I felt it was as much my responsibility as theirs to try to find some common ground and establish rapport. I adopted that philosophy so I wouldn't constantly have to be angry. Quite honestly, sometimes I'd worry that I wasn't getting through to them."

But before long it was clear that at least some of the pigtail dunkers turned into mentors. "Some of these fellow salespeople turned out to be my strong supporters in a year as well as friends, people to whom I could go and ask, 'Hey I'm having trouble with this account, what should I do?' "

Dealing with Customers as "The First Female Salesperson"

Before long, Faunce discovered that she wasn't just shattering misconceptions within her own work environment about what kind of jobs women can do but apparently setting a precedent within her field.

"I found out that I was the first female to sell computer systems in the newspaper industry as a whole. While there were other women selling equipment such as typesetters, none had sold computer systems."

So she learned to get used to gapes when she walked into the production areas with their giant clanging presses and ink-stained pressmen, where virtually the only other females in the buildings were gracing the Snap-on Tools calendars. "The newspaper industry was very chauvinistic, particularly in the production area. I used to walk in to a production director's office and he would look at me and literally say, 'Where's the salesperson?'

Once Faunce set her potential client straight that *she* was the salesperson, "I'd have to answer 20 questions about newspapers and computers."

Faunce also discovered that it's one thing to know your stuff and another to do something a man can't.

"At one point when I was helping my regional manager pack up a system at a demo we were doing at a customer site, I noticed he was trying to put the keyboard into the wrong box. When I told him, 'No, that's not the way it goes' and showed him how to do it, the customer's retort was, 'Are you good at this because you pack your husband's shirts?' to the at-that-point unmarried Faunce.

Faunce recognizes that it's not always possible to teach old boys new tricks—and it's risky business if the old boy is your customer—so she bit her tongue. "This guy was close to 60 years old and as far as I'm concerned, I'm not going to change him. As long as somebody's just ignorant and not rude, there's no sense making an issue of their behavior."

The second test Faunce had to pass was how much alcohol she could hold. While Faunce was adept at answering tough technical questions, artificing a wooden leg required a different kind of finesse. On one meeting with a hard-drinking client, "I was literally pouring these stingers into this plant next to the table. I had no choice: I'd say 'No, thank you' each time he'd order me a drink but he'd keep ordering them anyway and I didn't want the atmosphere to get adversarial. But I knew if I had too many—the drink was Courvoisier, straight up—I'd end up flat on my butt."

The third test, which Faunce's male colleagues didn't have to pass, was whether you could resist a client who wants to mix pleasure with business and still make the sale. Faunce had to meet this challenge at the tender age of 24.

Faunce was negotiating a contract with a client at dinner

at a restaurant on an out-of-town trip when the man first propositioned her—although it was more of a statement of intent than a proposal.

"He basically informed me that he was going to take me to bed. I said, 'Well I don't think so' and I changed the subject. Then I dropped my fork."

For the next two hours, Faunce was able to keep the conversation concentrated on business, or at least steer it in that direction. But when it was time to wrap up the meeting, the moment of truth came: Much as she might have wanted to beat a hasty retreat, the man was her only source of transportation to the hotel.

"So he's dropping me off at my hotel and I try to get out of the car and I say 'Good night.' Then he gets out of the car and he says, 'I'm coming in with you.'

Faunce's heart leapt to her throat. "I said 'No, that's not necessary.' He says 'No, I insist.' And he gets out of the car and gets my bags.

"My brain is thinking, 'How the hell do I get out of this one?' And I'm checking into the hotel, with him still holding my bag."

Faunce once again tried the polite-but-firm approach to dissuade the man, to no avail. "I say, 'Thank you' and I reach for my bag and he reaches for the key and gets it. So now I'm in the elevator with him and I can't believe this is happening. At this point I'm sort of in shock. I'm realizing now I'm in deep trouble and I'm thinking to myself, 'You stupid fool, what are you going to do next?' "

Once they got to the door of her hotel room, however, Faunce knew exactly what to do next: throw diplomacy to the winds.

"I told him to give me back my key. And I started screaming—I just went nuts—and I called him every name in the book. I think I probably used the word 'asshole' a few times.

"And it worked. I slammed the door, locked it and cried all night long."

Needless to say, Faunce was prepared to forfeit the sale since she had no intentions of sacrificing her integrity to get it. Ultimately, she was able to keep both.

"The next day I had a meeting with the guy and he said, not wanting to lose face, of course, 'So are you in a better mood today?' "

Faunce didn't miss a beat. "I said, 'Yes—as long as you behave yourself, I think we can probably proceed,' and that was it. We went right along and I got the deal."

What's more, Faunce continued to do business with the man, but on her terms. "He didn't try it again. I made sure of that: I always managed to have somebody else with me every time I met with him—a guy, needless to say, a big guy. And he never tried it again."

Faunce says that working women don't have many options when confronted with sexual harassment from a customer; you're forced to at least try to reason with the individual before resorting to confrontation because your primary responsibility is to make the sale.

"In the beginning you try to find ways to avoid the conflict; you try to put down the behavior without 'slamming it.' I'd head it off and then I'd talk business and I'd think, 'Okay, I put it down.' And an hour later he'd bring the subject up again. It's when you reach the point two hours later when you realize diplomacy is not going to work, then you say, 'Screw you. Get out of my face.'

Why Sales Is a Great Arena for Women

Apart from those occasions when you have to fend off customers whose hormones are in overdrive, Faunce maintains that being a woman can be an advantage in a sales environment.

"I used to get introduced, 'This is our salesperson, isn't she prettier than yours?' As a result, I'd get more time with the client than the guys would."

What's more, since women generally have to outperform men to get noticed, sales is a concrete, measurable way to show your management that you're an asset to the bottom line.

"Selling certainly is a way that you can prove your credentials because it's fairly black and white: you either make a sale or you don't—you either achieve quota or you don't."

Sales is also the fastest way to learn your business, Faunce says, since you'll only succeed in winning over a customer if you know your product inside and out.

"You have to be able to grasp some pretty complex computer concepts, understand the requirements of your customer and be able to present a solution to their business problems in plain English."

But the real heady rewards are that once you've sold the system you make money—big money.

"This was not nickel-and-dime stuff where you had to sell 52 units a month to make quota; in selling your account you're practically managing a little business. We were selling large-scale $2–3 million systems to major newspapers.

For five consecutive years Faunce vindicated her mentor's faith in her talents as a saleswoman—and left her detractors in the dust. She led Atex's sales force as a top performer, averaging more than $5 million in revenues each year and at the same time increasing Atex's market share in New England and eastern Canada by a whopping 300 percent.

Like most successful women, Faunce maintains that women can never afford either to rest on their laurels or to count on their mentors to give them a leg up on the ladder. Instead, they need to be proactive in "managing" their careers, whether that means gaining a breadth of experience in other areas or getting their feet wet in management.

Why Women Should Look for Turnaround Opportunities

In 1985, Faunce decided it was time to expose herself to more of Atex's product line and thereby broaden her opportunities for advancement, so she moved out of direct sales into a job as manager of sales support in the company's marketing services area. Her responsibilities included setting up product demonstrations and writing proposals for the company's entire product line. The move paid off in the form of two successive promotions: to Director of Marketing Services in 1986 and to National Accounts Director for the legal market in 1987.

In her capacity as national accounts director, Faunce was asked by the president of Atex to analyze whether the company should stay in the legal market, since it had always played a lesser role in the company's customer base. As a result of her optimistic projections for the market's growth, the unit was carved out into a separate division called Kodak Legal Systems and subsequently incorporated as a subsidiary in July 1990. Faunce not only showed senior management that Kodak ought to stay in the business but continued to break sales records as an executive. "Our first sale was the largest in the legal systems industry in the last 10 years: over a $10 million dollar deal."

At a Career Crossroads

But then the boom fell in January 1990 when management decided that, stellar track record or no, the future looked dim for law firm information management systems and they eliminated Faunce's unit.

No, Faunce doesn't blame management for not forewarning her that her unit was on the critical list. "In the four years that KLS was in existence there were five occasions where management told me, 'We're not sure that KLS is a strategic fit and we might shut you down.' Kodak is restructuring and concentrating on its 'strategic intent,' which is electronic imaging. And law firm information systems don't fall into that category." So she hadn't been left out of the "loop" by the men in charge.

Nor does Faunce feel that she was singled out for unfair treatment because of her sex, given that some of the highly placed male mentors who assisted her ascent into management met with the same fate. "In the last year or so all of my 'backers' have now left the company. They wound up either finding jobs elsewhere or taking early retirement."

And not having backers is a more ominous development in a woman's career than losing her status, Faunce declares. "At the same time my unit was eliminated, I was facing the fact that there was nobody left on the inside who had a personal investment in me. And you need to have people above you in the hierarchy who will continue to sing your praises. Otherwise, everybody's very 'nice' to you, but . . . In the last year, I have interviewed 18 people within Kodak to find a job and everybody gave me their time but that's it."

Nancy Faunce maintains that her dilemma is simply the gender-neutral fallout of corporate politics: the phenomenon that occurs when a new regime takes power, it awards the plum jobs to long-time allies while the holdovers from the old administration—the unfamiliar faces—have to sink or swim on their own. Even a superlative track record like Faunce's became an Orwellian nonevent in this new reality.

"There's a phenomenon in corporate life—which blows my mind—in which management says that what you've accomplished in the past may be relevant, but it's 'not relevant to me.' It's sort of, 'What have you done for me *lately*?' All people know is that Kodak Legal Systems was shut down and I was associated with it. So I wouldn't say it was a black mark against me but it's a grey mark."

Sizing up some of Faunce's career choices, some Monday-morning quarterbackers with more of a team-player mentality might say that she would still be in the winner's circle today had she spent more time scheming to save her hide than she spent running her business. But that's not Faunce's view.

"Sure, I could have 'saved my career' had I shifted from a results-oriented approach to more of a political approach. I could have played a 'big-company game' and started cultivating new power brokers when I saw that all my power brokers were on their way out. Do I wish I had done that? No.

"Because in doing so I would have had to take valuable time from running the company, which was my job, to do something personal for my career. My bottom line is that if you're going to be a business manager you have to do what's right for the business."

Faunce points out that if she had heeded the advice of team-player types when she was offered the opportunity to head up KLS in the first place, she would have turned it down—and passed up the career opportunity of a lifetime.

"There were people who said I was demoted by getting the legal market assignment, not because it was a turnaround situation but because the product wasn't the company's main line of business. I saw it instead as a challenge. Let's face it, there's a difference between basic folks in this world; there are those who are willing to take risks, who've got the guts to take a chance and risk failure and there are others who prefer to take the safe route."

Faunce insists that her experience hasn't soured her on corporate life, it's only vindicated her skeptical view of "big-company" culture, where personal agendas often take priority over what's best for the business.

"When you're an employee of a small start-up company, management doesn't care what you look like, they just want to get the work done. In a competitive environment, the fact that there's plenty of work creates opportunities for everybody. It's almost as if being in a 'busy mode' is an equalizing factor in the workplace.

"But in larger companies you've got a lot of personal agendas. Because large companies are too big to mean anything, because they're bigger than people who work for them, individuals can afford to follow their own personal agendas even if it's not to the good of the company."

When the boom fell, Faunce was given two options: she could take a year's severance package if she couldn't find another comparable job within Kodak in the Boston area. Or she could accept a "maybe later" position that was essentially an individual contributor's job with an unwritten promise that it would lead to a management post.

Faunce's initial choice in April 1991 was to take the second option "because the conventional wisdom is that it's easier to find a job if you currently have a job." For ten months she swam in corporate purgatory, trying to convince her ego that her career prospects would magically reverse yet again to what they were before the "fall" in 1988. But her gut was wrenched daily by the reality of being a nonperson.

"Kodak's new management team offered me the job of strategic alliance director for a new program: desktop color software, and told me I'd be made manager. But they wouldn't put it in writing. And then they started interviewing people to work in the department. I would ask, 'Excuse me, aren't these people going to work for me?' Then I found out they were making offers to people I hadn't even interviewed. The experience directly undermined my self-confidence. It's not that they don't value me; they like me because I can produce. But I'm not on the first team; not in the inner circle."

Faunce admits that during this limbo period she wasted time and emotional energy downsizing her professional esteem to match the new political reality, rather than accepting the situation for what it was and making a clean break. The experience is not unlike languishing in a going-nowhere romantic relationship and making excuses for trying to make it work, Faunce says—an exercise in futility women engage in all too often.

"When you're in a bad relationship you tell yourself that if you work hard enough you can make it work. If you do this, that, and the other thing it will change. But then once you leave the relationship and do all the grieving you look back and you say, 'Is that me that was so stupid? Why didn't I just walk out?' Now having had a chance to take a breather from this whole thing, I can now say, 'This is crap.' "

What's worse, even when her psyche was healed sufficiently to make a clean break emotionally, the "microeconomic" reality in Faunce's household forced her to physically remain at Kodak nonetheless, at least temporarily.

"I recently learned that Atex, where my husband works, is downsizing again and he's going to be on the list of that now rare species: middle management. So as a family unit, we are trying to sort out what makes the most sense: both of us unemployed and job hunting or one of us still earning benefits and the like. But as of today, Kodak has not agreed to give me my severance package or to give me a job that is acceptable to me."

In October 1991 Faunce was considering a number of career options, including teaming up with one of her former mentors to form a systems integration company servicing large companies. Faunce also happens to believe that the entrepreneurial environment is not only a healthier one for women, it's better for business.

"I happen to think that what's going to take the United States forward in the next 10 years are the small companies who in essence help companies get their jobs done more effectively. You can see that going on in the computer industry today: companies such as IBM are making deals with all these small outfits in order to better meet their customer needs."

Faunce says her bottom line is that career success has to be based on whether you're living up to your own goals as a human being, not how skillful or lucky you are at hitching yourself to the right star.

"You have got to pick your own shots, you have to live by your own yardstick. And if you live by other people's yardsticks you're never going to make it because everybody's going to change it on you."

chapter 7

Loraine Binion
of Levi Strauss & Co.:

THE DOUBLE DISADVANTAGE: DEALING WITH SEX AND RACE DISCRIMINATION

As a minority woman, Loraine Binion faced a variety of obstacles climbing the corporate ladder to her current post as Manager of Internal Audit for San Francisco-based Levi Strauss & Co. One of them she narrowly escaped was being pushed off the first rung as a newly minted CPA and college graduate.

One of Binion's first bosses attempted to lay her off in favor of a white male whom he admitted was less capable and had less seniority than she.

His rationale: "He told me he would let me go because as a black woman I was more marketable on the outside; I could probably find a job more quickly than this guy. And the guy needed the job more."

Suspecting that what her boss was attempting was against the law besides being unfair, she complained to the company's personnel department.

"They said, 'Let's see about that,' and I was picked up by another manager," Binion said. "I did have some allies. It's important to have allies in the company."

Binion said she had a premonition that her boss was not comfortable working with her before the axe started to fall, because she had been at a party with his wife "and after she had had a couple of glasses of wine she decided she would ask me all the questions that she wanted to ask about Black people. She asked me, 'How can you be comfortable in your work environment with all whites? If I were in an environment with all Black people I'd be totally nervous.' And we talked and talked and about 45 minutes later I said to her, 'You know what the problem is? You're uncomfortable because I *am* comfortable being here. I don't go to work every day thinking, 'Oh, she's a white person, he's a white person.'

"And when I went back to work I thought to myself, this man is married to this woman so obviously he must share some of her views."

Binion, who also has an MBA from UCLA, came to Levi Strauss in 1979 after working for Arthur Andersen for three years. Nine years later she was made controller of a $100 million subsidiary, Brittania Sportswear, and was promoted to Manager of Corporate Audit for all of Levi Strauss in August of 1991.

While almost losing her job in the early part of her career wasn't the only obstacle Binion has had to face climbing the ladder to management, she feels that the other discouragements have been more "noise in the system" than daunting challenges.

"Sure, I've run into people who aren't very enlightened or even ones who have tried to sideswipe me. But in my opinion these have been small annoyances that I've been able to overcome."

What to Do When Job Competition Heats Up: Network, Network, Network

Binion's strategy to sidestep the sideswipers in the corporation is to ally herself with the political heavyweights and maintain high visibility, a gambit she says men and women must play in today's downsizing-driven environment.

"Being smart isn't cutting it anymore; there are plenty of smart people in the workplace. Thanks to the baby boom, there are a lot of good candidates for management jobs. Everyone knows a lot of middle management people who are either unemployed, out of work or underemployed. So there's a lack of upward movement that is not race- or gender-driven, it's just pure economics."

Binion predicts that the stiff competition for fewer slots will create a white male backlash if women and minorities are perceived as receiving special treatment. "A lot of majority males here who've been at the company for awhile resent the fact that Levi Strauss is trying to show sensitivity to the diversified work force, the fact that it's trying to move more women and minorities up to the senior ranks. That situation is not good for me, but it has forced me to create more opportunities for myself. Once you establish a credibility level, and you've got a strong resume and you've developed important contacts it's a little easier to get ahead. If you haven't done that it's hard as hell."

But wait a minute. Isn't doing all this playing politics, a game that meritocracy-seeking women will find distasteful? Binion maintains that if you don't play the game you'll lose it.

"The definition of politics is using influence and relationships to get a desired result. So politics do not have to be negative as long as they don't work to the detriment of someone else. Almost all business in most societies throughout the world is conducted by forming relationships with others. Successful women know this. Men have always known it.

"Let's face it, if you don't promote yourself, no one else is going to. If you want to dance, you better get up and tap your feet—no one's going to ask you to dance if you just sit on the sidelines. This is real-world reality."

Find a Mentor—Or Two

Binion says that it's crucial to find a mentor—the more the merrier—to maximize your chances that when management slots are discussed, your name will get suggested at least once. Finding a mentor isn't that difficult, she avers.

"You'll notice somebody when you're at lunch or you'll run into them at a meeting and you call them up afterward and say, 'I heard you say this at the meeting, it sounds interesting. Can you tell me more about it, would you mind giving me some help?' Or, 'Could we meet for coffee, I'd like to get to know this area better?' There's half a dozen ways to do it.

"You show an interest in the person's responsibilities and you ask for advice. Older men have an ego and they like acting as big brothers and giving advice. You talk to two or three different people—you don't put all your eggs in one basket. Some people will be receptive, others will put you off. If they do, you just try to find somebody else."

Once you find a mentor, make sure to thank him or her for his or her help, Binion advises. "When they do something nice, you send them a little note, you remember to send them a card at Christmas time."

Don't count on your mentor to help you leapfrog over other candidates, Binion warned. She says the era in which you could find a powerful ally who could pull strings doesn't exist any more, if it ever did.

"Ten and twenty years ago we heard about people having mentors who pulled them up through the organization but that kind of individual attention doesn't exist: no single individual can call the shots and pull you up over other people. Individuals fall in and out of favor."

But don't discount the effect that your cheering section can have when it comes time for management to winnow the choices for a top job.

"If you can impress these people to speak well of you, there will be someone other than your boss who can say 'I know the right person for this job' when a promotion opportunity comes up."

Dealing with Sexual Harassment—With Diplomacy or Directness

Just take care that in the course of cultivating a mentor your overtures don't send a mixed message, Binion cautions, because most men "just don't understand" that a woman's appeal for sponsorship is not a mating call in disguise. Binion had to confront precisely this dilemma during a business trip with her boss early in her career.

"As we were eating dinner, he came right out and asked me to go to his hotel room. I told him very straightforwardly that I had just gotten married and wasn't interested in a romantic relationship. And that I thought it would damage our professional relationship. Fortunately, that's all it took to nip in the bud any romantic fantasies he might have. And after we got back into the office things were fine."

Binion admits that the incident didn't take her by surprise because the man had been putting the moves on her for several months back at the office. "He would always put his hand on my shoulder and give me a pat. Or he would take opportunities to push up against me. He even took me to meet his mother when we were traveling."

Binion says women should at least try the diplomatic approach to squelching these unwanted advances before resorting to a direct one—particularly if your career is at stake. Binion says that because women have to temper their outrage at such violations with a long view toward job security she can relate to the predicament of Professor Anita F. Hill, who made headlines in late 1991 when she alleged that then Supreme Court Justice nominee Clarence Thomas had sexually harassed her 10 years earlier but she seemingly didn't take bold steps to combat the overtures.

"I felt that I had to grin and bear the situation because I didn't know what his reaction would be. Here I was, twenty-seven years old at the time; I needed all the support I could get. And here he was, a white, male manager who had taken an interest in me, whom I believed could do a lot of things for me. That's why I can understand where Anita Hill was coming from. On the other hand, when push came to shove I knew I could take him to task."

The depth of a woman's courage to defend her self-respect at the risk of jeopardizing her career is directly proportional to her breadth of on-the-job training, Binion maintains. "Our ability to react is based on our knowledge and our experience base. At thirty-eight years old I'm very sure of myself now but eleven years ago I didn't have the savvy or the strength or the maturity or the comfort level to handle these experiences in the same way. Maturity is a big factor in not only your ability to take action but to accept the consequences of the action."

Commanding Respect from Employees Who Question Her Authority

Binion is among the elite two percent of corporate executives who are minorities, but still she must constantly defend her position to males outside her direct scope of authority who simply can't reconcile it with their image of what women can do.

As manager of corporate internal audit—the first woman in the company's history to hold this position—Binion heads up a staff of auditors who travel the world scrutinizing the books of various Levi facilities. After her staff completes their reports, Binion meets with the managers of each facility and makes recommendations for changing certain procedures, such as cash management, dealings with contractors, and payroll arrangements. The job isn't an easy one irrespective of gender; the audit is virtually the corporate equivalent of undergoing an IRS audit, and no one welcomes it.

"I go out to a lot of factories, plants, and sales offices that are run by guys in their 50s and early 60s who have been with the company for 20 and 30 years, longer than I've been alive as they love to tell me. Suddenly these good old boys from the South who run their shop like it's been *their* shop have to deal with a young Black woman from San Francisco who is telling them that what they're doing is not correct.

"My authority and knowledge are constantly challenged. They will say, 'I don't believe you or I don't trust you' when I advise them about new procedures to follow. I had a big confrontation recently with one facility manager who was being argumentative for the sake of being so. I finally told him with just a hint of sarcasm, 'This conversation is very stimulating. However, we are going nowhere. I suggest we get on with business because you're not acting in an appropriate manner.' "

The man ultimately came around to Binion's way of thinking the next day without actually conceding. "He gave me a watered down 'semiapology.' "

But Binion doesn't expect contriteness from male subordinates who ultimately see the error of their ways. Just results.

"I cannot change their behavior, I can only demand their respect. But I can only do that by going through their charade.

And I expect I will confront this behavior in the field for another year or two until they get a chance to know who I am. I'm getting used to it now. The more you go through these verbal exercises, the sharper your skills are, the more you can add to your 'portfolio.' I'm becoming more seasoned."

Binion avers that much of a woman's ability to prevail over Neanderthalism in the course of man-to-woman "combat" comes not from slick negotiating tactics, clever put-downs, or psychological warfare but by simply willing yourself to be successful.

"A lot of the way people react to you is based on the way you present yourself, the way you come across to them. You have to deal from a position of strength. Some women need assertiveness training. Not everyone has the ability to do it on her own."

On the other hand, Binion says that many women already inherently manifest many of the management qualities that are required by the leaders of the twenty-first century's diverse workforce.

"Along with being a visionary, a true leader has strong communication skills, including listening skills, is a motivator and a team player, gives quality feedback to her subordinates, and celebrates their successes. The stereotypical male autocratic leadership style of the 1960s is not acceptable in today's companies or with the workforce of today and tomorrow."

Sara Westendorf
of Hewlett-Packard:

GETTING THE PASSWORD TO THE MEN'S CLUB

When you're female, nice-looking, and work in an all-male environment, you can expect to endure some nudge-nudge, wink-wink ogling from the guys. Sara Westendorf's approach is to nudge-nudge, wink-wink, ogle right back.

As one of the first female design engineers hired by Hewlett-Packard in 1976, Westendorf had plenty of gawking to deal with—not to mention snide remarks about entering wet T-shirt contests. But Westendorf says, "I'll often act like guys are only a sex object; their body, hairiness, and good looks are more important than anything else. There are guys I'll call honey and sweetheart, sugar pie and all this."

Sound like reverse macho? Not if you consider the context. As laboratory manager overseeing 140 engineers who design diagnostic systems for cars and aircraft, Westendorf's work environment is closer to the rough-and-tumble factory floor than a straight-jacketed office setting.

Her situation is not unlike the lone female fire fighter on the force or carpenter on a construction site: she must not only command her colleague's respect by excelling at 'men's work,' but also win their friendship so that they don't have to behave as if "there's a lady present." For Westendorf, humor isn't used as a weapon to prevail in a battle of wits but as a password to gain entry into the clubhouse.

"Being one of the guys, getting your humor on the same level—all that creates the environment where men feel they can

97

open up in front of you. You should make them feel that they can say exactly what they would say if there were only men in the room, even if it takes using the 'F'-word on occasion."

Being one of the guys isn't particularly daunting if you tend to prefer the company of men in the first place, says Westendorf. "Men are my best friends and I tend to share interests with them. I enjoy organizing poker games, playing basketball, going out for a beer."

What's more, Westendorf maintains that women who don't feel comfortable with men, who act uptight around the very male executives they seek as peers, often sabotage their own admission to the inner sanctum of management.

"I believe that women often create their own "glass ceiling" by alienating the very peers and superiors who will influence their promotion. Let's say a woman is going to talk with an HP Vice-President and she's the sort of person who gets flustered or offended at a dirty joke. It's going to make this guy uncomfortable. His reaction will be: 'I don't like dealing with these damned women, they're all upright.' "

Male Subordinates as Friends

Westendorf is proud to report that because she works hard at establishing trusting friendships with the men who work for her, she hasn't yet faced overt resentment from any of the men who have reported to her.

"I feel good about creating an environment where a guy feels he can be candid about any misgivings he might have. For example, I once offered a job to a guy who said he wanted some time to think it over. So to open him up I suggested we get together and talk about it and during this talk he said, 'Let me admit that my hesitancy is that I'm not sure I'd feel comfortable working for a woman.'

"My response was to tell him that I appreciated him being honest about it. Then I said, 'Here's a list of male managers who have worked for me whom you might want to touch base with.' So we talked it through, he wound up accepting the job and it worked out quite well. It's crucial to be proactive in creating an environment where guys can express their doubts like that."

This trusting relationship between herself and her staff paid off in a recent decision affecting customers, said Westendorf, when a group of managers who report to her were debating whether to put a woman in charge of a team of engineers to design a diagnostic system for Nissan.

"It is so key to Hewlett-Packard's strategy to be successful doing business with Japan. At the same time, it's widely known that the Japanese have a tough time accepting women in business, at least women in nonclerical positions. I'm grateful that these guys felt comfortable enough about expressing their doubts to ask me, 'Will the Japanese really accept a woman or shall we go for an all male team?' "

Not surprisingly, the group ultimately opted to choose a male leader because of the harsh reality of having to accommodate the less-enlightened Japanese business culture—instead of taking the "politically correct" but suicidal approach of tapping a woman to head the team.

Had Westendorf not established that comfort level with members of her staff and instead toed the ideological feminist line on the issue, the men would have probably tiptoed around the issue for fear of offending her.

"Then instead of being candid they would have had to fabricate other reasons why the women candidates wouldn't qualify. What's worse, they might have started believing those reasons."

Westendorf admits that not only did circumstances on this project prevent them from putting the female candidate in the leadership position but even Westendorf herself stayed in the background just to be safe, and she's the boss. But not for long, she vows.

"Once we earn Nissan's respect for our technical expertise and for the value-added qualities that Hewlett-Packard provides, then one of my guys can say, 'I'd like you to meet my boss.' Then I'll already have credibility with them because of the track record of the team working for me."

Earning Respect From an All-Male Customer Base

While doing business with the Japanese is a challenge for any woman, winning customer respect is a tricky business even domestically within the all-male grease monkey environment of the factory floor.

While a salesperson will most often make the initial contact with a potential customer for the services of Westendorf's group, which makes systems for manufacturers and dealers that pinpoint vehicle glitches, there's a limit to a salesperson's technical know-how. It's up to Westendorf and her team to close the deal.

When breaking the ice with these potential clients, Westendorf makes it clear from the get-go that she means fun as well as business. Westendorf offers the following example of her initial meeting with a potential customer, Mercedes Benz.

"Let's face it, when you go into these meetings everybody is sort of stiff and businesslike whether there's a woman in the room or not. So while we're introducing ourselves, I'll say in German 'Our first big decision is to figure out where you're going to go out on your first night in California.' So I'll get everybody psyched about where we're going to go out and make small talk, tell a few jokes about who likes what weird food. And then segue into business with, 'Now that we've gotten the important stuff decided, let's get down to business.'

"The bottom line is that when you're establishing a business relationship you're creating trust, and what matters first is getting that relationship established, even it's over something as seemingly trivial as picking a hot spot to go for lunch. You create an environment where they don't have to mind their Ps and Qs because there's a lady present."

Once the potential client is relaxed, step two is to convince him to take your authority and expertise seriously, Westendorf says. "So once I've convinced them that I'm an okay person who is not going to make them uptight, I will talk about previous projects I've managed in such a way to convey authority.

"I'll say, 'Back in the days when I was in charge of project thus-and-such, the technology was in its infancy and I had to assign 60 engineers just to get the first prototype up and running. Now, based on the technology we have in place today, I could potentially achieve three times the productivity with a team of 12 engineers designing the system for your factory.' "

Dealing With Other Departments

Meeting her business goals frequently requires obtaining data from other areas of the company where male managers are unfamiliar with her power. There's a special challenge for female executives in convincing others that she conveys authority. Because to many people, a woman's voice sounds like a secretary conveying her boss' message.

"Frequently developing the systems that my people design will depend on using a computer or an instrument from another division. Now, Hewlett-Packard's trade secrets, our product strategy, is all 'competitive edge.' If we have a state-of-the-art technology that could put us ahead of DEC or IBM we are very, very careful with whom we share that information. Let's say that we're designing a system that requires using a computer that a division in Colorado is developing that won't be introduced until 1993. If I were a man, I'd have instant credibility that enables me to have a discussion about this information with the man in charge of the project—whether he knows me or not. As a woman, I have to demonstrate the credibility that will allow him to open up with me.

"For example, if I were to call the lab manager in Colorado who doesn't know me from Eve and I use this breezy approach: 'Hi, I'm from Hewlett-Packard Sunnyvale and I'd like to find out what you're doing for your next-generation product development,' I would get nowhere fast. The guy on the other end of the line would probably think, 'Who is this bimbo whom I don't know from a hole in the wall asking me for proprietary information?' "

On the other hand, she says, she will get a lot further if her words contain both authority and data only an 'insider' would be privy to—not to mention conveying that she, too is a boss.

"For example, I'd make much more of an inroad if I used terminology describing certain hardware and software involved and said, 'We are using the computer you released last year and we really love your VXI strategy and the functionality of the instrument library. There's a lot of similarity between the work my team of 80 engineers is doing and what your lab is doing. Could you and I touch base on our next generation product plans because your work is such a cornerstone to our strategy?' "

Making Herself Indispensable

Westendorf made her ascent to management the same way most women earn their stripes, by working twice as hard as her male colleagues. A workaholic who thought nothing of putting in a couple of all-nighters at the office each week in addition to weekend work, Westendorf became known as a quick study who could make her boss' job easier by solving his toughest problems, while at the same time ensuring she got credit for the results.

"My secret to getting ahead has been to observe the toughest challenges my boss was wrestling with and start thinking about the issues that I had the wherewithal to solve. This works, of course, as long as I'm working for an open-minded boss who values the input of women.

"You walk up to your boss and say, 'You know, I've been thinking about this issue or challenge that we're facing. If you want to delegate the responsibility of solving that problem to me, I've got some good ideas and solutions.' You become known as his problem solver.

"When an opportunity comes up to go for a promotion, you can reiterate your contributions to your boss at that point, saying: 'Look at these tough issues we faced and here's what I was able to do to resolve them and be successful.' It really puts you in a good position."

Westendorf's first project at HP was on the design team for an input-output board for the HP 1000 A series, a design that's still in production.

"Because I was willing to try to get responsibility for taking on the toughest challenges, I got to design these four different circuit boards. It gives me a lot of pride to see that they're still being manufactured."

How to Spot a Neanderthal Boss

Of course, you can only become known as your boss' problem-solver if you work for a boss who values the input of women.

All too often, women sabotage their own career ascent by languishing in a dead end job situation, making excuses for working for an unenlightened boss rather than trading him in for a better boss. Westendorf credits her rapid rise as partly a result of her "radar" that can detect negative signals from closed-minded bosses.

"Since I've worked here I've had two bosses whom I'd qualify as belonging to the Neanderthal camp. And because I saw that they were not inclined to let me contribute at the level of my capabilities, I transferred out of these areas as soon as it was physically possible. In the first case I worked for the guy three weeks and the second, six months."

Westendorf says that the warning signs of Neanderthalism are that your boss simply is selectively deaf to your suggestions, while his hearing returns to normal when a man comes up with the same idea.

"I would make suggestions to this boss about doing such-and-such and he would totally brush it off; it would fall on deaf ears. The suggestion could range from something as trivial as taking a five-minute break during a meeting to scheduling a high-level conference with a customer over a certain issue. And a male manager—who reported to me, no less!—would come up and suggest the exact same thing to him and the response was, 'Oh, yes!'

"Well, that sort of thing didn't have to happen more than once or twice before I made the decision to get out. You say to yourself, 'Hey, wait a minute! That behavior doesn't make any sense.' "

Finding a Mentor

At the same time you side-step the land mine of reporting to a man who won't further your career, it's crucial to cultivate people in high places who will, Westendorf avers.

"Sure, women have to perform on the job and get the results that get them noticed, but it never hurts to develop a strong working relationship with somebody whose star is rising fast and who has a lot of credibility with the powers that be so that the next time management is looking for somebody to fill a higher slot they consider you."

The relationship typically starts with a request for advice. "The first time you're wrestling with an issue of any magnitude and an individual comes to mind whom you've observed in action—say, you liked the way he solved a technical problem or handled a customer—you might say something to him like, 'I saw your presentation on such and such. I was really impressed with the way you articulated the strategy. And right now I am facing a certain issue and I'd be interested in your thoughts on it.' "

The benefits are twofold, Westendorf says: You get valuable feedback that you can use in your work, and you have an ally who is familiar with your approach to problems.

How to Deal with Colleagues Who Don't Respect Your Ideas

Westendorf's strategy for neutralizing emotional, irrational men who don't respect her ideas is the time-honored tactic used by many men in dealing with women whom they perceive as emotional and irrational: Suggest that their hormones are raging out of control. But she does it in such a way to make allies out of the other men in the room, not just embarrass the perpetrator.

"Let's say there's a guy whom I've already observed is not supportive of women in technology or business, and he gets argumentative at a meeting, showing some emotion about some point that is opposite mine. What I'll do after he blows off steam is I'll say, 'What's the matter, Steve, is it that time of the month for you? Perhaps we should wait a week until you're in a better mood so that you can discuss this matter rationally.'

"Although I make a remark that sounds flippant or sarcastic I keep the hostile tone out of it. The remark is designed to get a laugh and usually does get a laugh out of eighty percent of the people in the room—*and* the guy who was over-emotional gets the message."

Exchanges such as the one cited above in which a male

colleague will challenge a woman head-on are rare, however. Men more typically will either ignore a woman's idea or co-opt it.

"If I find myself in a meeting in which every time I make a point I get interrupted, as if my opinion isn't worthy, I'll just take charge of the whole meeting. I'll stand up, walk to the front of the room and say, 'I need your attention, the point I'm making is really important. And I think the approach you're taking to this business problem is barking up the wrong tree.' I don't let them ignore me."

But women have to be judicious about how they handle males who treat them like the invisible woman, varying their tactics according to whether the perpetrator is acting out of mere ignorance or sheer hostility.

Westendorf recounts an example of a male boss who unwittingly permitted a colleague of hers to usurp credit for her idea. Rather than confronting either her colleague or her boss directly, she instead chose to broach the subject to her boss in private and he owned up to the error.

"On this occasion, I brought up an idea in a meeting, it was ignored, then the marketing manager brought up the identical idea and my boss said, 'Oh, that's a great idea.' I didn't say anything in the meeting, but after it was over I asked my boss if I could talk to him privately for a minute. And I explained to him that I felt that the marketing manager got credit for my idea when the recognition should have been mine. He apologized and thanked me for bringing it to his attention."

"When an issue arises, I believe in confronting it head-on on a one-on-one basis. If something happens that is not right, I don't let it fester. My boss made a mistake but he admitted he made a mistake and he hasn't done it again."

Managing a Diverse Work Environment

While Westendorf says she has benefited from mentoring advice during the course of her career, she's now at a position near the narrow peak of the leadership pyramid where her white, male superiors don't always have sufficient experience in managing a mixed-race, mixed-sex environment to be able to give her meaningful direction.

"The business environment of today is much more culturally diverse within the lower levels of the company than twenty years ago when the white, male vice-presidents of this company were at that level as engineers and first-level managers. So, in my responsibilities I've not only got to figure out how to manage huge business issues but be sensitive to the people-management issues in a culturally diverse environment.

"For example, I have two managers reporting to me who don't see eye-to-eye on a major strategic issue and one of them happens to be Black. They're very professional and gentlemanly to each other when they're in the same room, but if you get either one of them alone each will say the other one's incompetent. And it's impossible for people to solve a technical or a business problem if they don't have personal trust in each other and feel comfortable working together as a team.

"This is a situation in which I feel that it would be futile for me to ask my superiors for advice. While my bosses pay lip service to the concept of Affirmative Action, I don't think they know what it means to manage a culturally diverse workforce. Of course, all of us are at the bottom of the learning curve in this area, but the higher you go in the management chain the less experience you find."

Following in Mom's Footsteps

The dilemma of having few trusted allies to turn to for help in dealing with certain management issues is particularly thorny for Westendorf because unlike some of the other women profiled in this book, Westendorf didn't marry a man who wound up as her mentor.

"My exhusband didn't turn out to be as 'liberated' as I thought when I married him. It is hard to find a guy who can deal with a woman who earns $140,000 a year. Maybe they think they can in the beginning of the relationship but it eats away at them."

Fortunately, Westendorf can still rely on the support and

counsel of her Dad, David Dickinson, who was the "man be-hind" her mother, Alice Dickinson, an engineer-by-training turned academic who had the more important career in their two-career household.

Westendorf's Dad was the one who convinced his future wife that, over her own father's protestations, a mind like hers belonged on the job solving problems, not at home.

"When my father asked my mother to get married, he then asked, 'If we got married would you want to quit your job and stay home?' and she said, 'Yes.'

"So he said, 'Okay, I guess I won't be proposing to you.'

Apparently Alice Dickinson was so shell-shocked by this show of support she didn't quite know how to react. "A couple of dates later she asked him, 'You mean you really wouldn't mind if I built a career?'

"He told her, 'No, you're the most intelligent woman I've ever met and you've got a super future and it would be stupid for you to quit.'"

Alice Dickinson's career took off during World War II, when a "manpower" shortage forced America's corporate establish-ment to draw on the talents of its distaff population. But unlike many Rosie the Riveters of her era who were "drafted" onto factory floors, Dickinson was a college-educated career engineer who had been snubbed by some of the very companies who were tripping over each other to hire Westendorf 30 years later.

"When my mother first got out of college and she was trying to get a job as an engineer she couldn't even get an interview," Westendorf said. "Exactly 30 years later when I was getting my engineering degree, the same company that would not even talk to her would wind up calling me and say, 'Gee, you have a straight A average and that's wonderful and we'd like to explore these wonderful career opportunities in our company.' It was hard for me to even want to talk to people like that after they wouldn't even talk to my mother."

Dickinson nonetheless went on to achieve recognition in the private sector, ultimately choosing to switch to academia because she preferred the lifestyle.

Dickinson was working in a radiation research lab on a joint venture between MIT and Sperry Corp during World War II when she met Westendorf's father. "Ultimately they decided to go back and get their Ph.D.s and become professors because they liked the lifestyle: They liked having summers off and traveling." Dickinson worked her way up from math professor to chairman of the math department to dean of Smith College.

Westendorf is grateful to have been raised in an "equal opportunity" environment in which her parents had the same high expectations of her as they did her brother: "I had an androgynous upbringing where there was little to no stereotyping."

Westendorf maintains that it was important for her to have parents who not only assumed she was intelligent but also encouraged her to make her own playthings rather than buy them. This enabled Westendorf to develop the mechanical skills so sorely lacking in most women.

"As professors, my parents didn't earn a whole lot of money; we never bought a new car, we never bought any furniture. So if we wanted something we had to build it. When my brother and I wanted a boat, my parents said, 'Great. Go build it.' So we found some old wood in the barn and we had to figure out how to make it into a boat and how to waterproof it. When we formed a group to give plays, it was 'Great. Build your theater.' So we wired the barn with these spotlights. It really laid the background for what I needed to become an engineer."

Because her parents loved to travel abroad, Westendorf also learned how to fend for herself in unfamiliar surroundings. "Any opportunity my parents could get jobs as visiting professors at an overseas university, why we'd pack up and go off. We spent a total of five years abroad: in England, India, Switzerland, France, and Germany."

Choosing a "Man's" Career

Seeing how "the other half lives" also pushed Westendorf onto an initial career path of trying to remedy social problems rather than ironing the glitches out of advanced technology. So after getting her Bachelor's degree from the University of Rochester, Westendorf pursued a Master's degree in social work at Rutgers University in her quest to help less fortunate people.

She worked for a county welfare department and for a family service agency in New Jersey while she was getting her degree. But she quit four months before she would have earned her MSW after discovering during her "on-the-job training" that she'd rather be paid well to solve problems than eke out an existence never solving them—doing "women's work."

"The social work classes were 98 percent women. The work paid barely minimum wage. And the people who had worked in it awhile were really frustrated and burned out."

It didn't take Westendorf long to see why. "When I was a caseworker in New Brunswick I had a family with 14 dependents under the age of 15. You get one kid to go to school for a whole week and three others drop out. It was absolutely impossible."

Westendorf started asking herself why she was working so hard for so little payback.

"At that time, my husband, who was studying engineering at Princeton, was being paid $100 a day to do consulting. When I was in social work school at Rutgers, not only did we not get paid for our field work, we had to pay tuition to get coached on it! So here's a woman in graduate school having to pay for the experience and a man in graduate school getting income for his experience. And having fun!

"And it hit me: I realized social work was an absolutely low-paid, futile, and burns-you-out "woman's" career while engineering was a high-paid "man's" career where you could see results. Engineering problems may seem tough or difficult to deal with, but at least there is a solution."

So she traded in her social work career for one in engineering, following in her Mom's footsteps after all.

Before Dickinson died in 1987, she and her daughter would compare notes on what it was like to be a woman in a man's world.

"She had to deal with management issues, too, because as Dean of the Smith faculty during the early 1970s all of the chairs of the various departments reported to her. She had some incredible issues to deal with: sexual harassment, age and sex discrimination in granting tenure, and she and I would talk these things over.

"I think it was my mother who taught me that before you can solve a problem you've got to force all of the issues out on the table, you can't let people hold their cards close to their chests. Those concepts I believe I got from her."

"But the same way my dad was the one who was in the

background for my mother, 'stoking the fire' for her throughout her career, he's done the same thing for me. I know he's really proud of me."

Prospects for Women *Are* Improving

Westendorf believes in a "trickle up" theory when it comes to women breaking management barriers; the higher women rise in management, the farther up the ceiling goes.

"Yes, the glass ceiling does exist, but I have seen the work environment get a whole lot better for women in the 15 years I've been in industry. As women start moving to the top and start being recognized for their outstanding contributions, this ceiling inches up."

"When I started here in 1976, it seemed then that one percent of the engineers were women and now it's 15 to 20 percent. I was the first woman in the company to be made R&D lab manager in 1984 and a week later another woman got promoted to that level. Today there's probably better than a dozen women lab managers. So I believe the job I hold is above the 'glass ceiling' that existed a decade ago.

"When management picks somebody for a top executive position, much of their judgement is influenced by their image of the people who would be successful there. And you usually picture a successful white male, just because the last three guys in that job were white males. Each level has to pick from the level below it to promote someone. You go one step at a time.

"Between my level of Lab Manager and President of the company there are three levels: Division Manager, Group Manager, and Sector Manager. Right now there are two female division managers who could be candidates for Group Managers, who head up an entity that has better than $100 million in revenues and overseeing a minimum of 500 people. However, among Sector Managers, the next level up, there are no female candidates to choose from."

Westendorf knows that she will have to put in a lot more time before the glass ceiling has inched up high enough for her to be considered for the CEO's job; she'd have to put in at least

two years in every position for each one of the three more promotions she'd need to head a $13 billion company.

"I don't know yet if I'd like to be CEO because I'm at least
10 years away from it—I've put 15 years into Hewlett-Packard
and it's been rewarding but within the next decade the time
may come to do something different with my life.

"If the opportunity presented itself and it seemed like the
right thing, I'd do it but I'm not going to bust my butt going
for it. Right now my job is a lot of fun but when it gets frustrating I sometimes think: 'Wow! Maybe there is life after Hewlett-Packard and what's that going to be?' I have thought that
I don't want to put another two and a half decades into HP."

chapter 9

Melissa Cadet
of River West Developments:
FINDING SUCCESS OUTSIDE THE FORTUNE 500

Growing up in the 1960s as one of a handful of minorities in a lily white Sacramento Catholic school, Melissa Cadet learned first hand what white women rarely discover until they enter the workforce: that certain classes of people are "more equal" than others.

"The nun who taught my second grade class simply would not give me the grades I deserved. The most devastating put-down were the grades on my book reports. I was a voracious reader and would turn in 32 three-or-four page reports over a six month period and only get Bs while others who would turn in three or four book reports that were two to three paragraphs in length would get As."

What tipped Cadet off to the fact that her teacher was exhibiting racial bias? Because the nun didn't simply ignore Cadet's achievement, she'd deny it—the same way some men deny the achievements of exceptional women by downgrading them to their perception of the rule.

"The nun came right out and accused me of having my parents do the reports for me, which didn't make sense because I did outstanding work in the classroom," Cadet recalls.

When Cadet tearfully recounted the teacher's allegations to her mother—herself unable to pursue a teaching career because of backward attitudes about minorities—she'd gently encourage her daughter to persevere.

"My Mom would say, 'Forget about the grade, look at what you're learning. Look at what you're getting out of the experience: you're turning into a better reader than anybody else. So go on and do the best you can do and enjoy yourself.' And at the end of the year I wound up getting the reading award after all."

Cadet's second encounter with racism occurred only eight years later when as a 10th grader she was passed over for selection as a foreign exchange student. This time she was better prepared to grab victory from the jaws of defeat. The following year she applied again, but also applied "diplomatic" pressure to the committee members to ensure they knew another "no" answer simply wasn't acceptable.

"I told the director of the program that I really didn't understand why I wasn't accepted the previous year. Restating my credentials, I said, 'I have a 4.0 average, I am President of the student body, I was elected to the student senate during my sophomore and junior year, and I'm a cheerleader. I certainly have the qualifications. Could I be filling out my application improperly or incorrectly?' "

Apparently because they were made "painfully aware" of her superior qualifications, the committee members had little choice but to accept her the second time. "I just resolved that I was going to overcome this barrier; that I was going to do whatever it took to achieve my objectives. And not only did I get my school's nomination but won the regional and national competition, becoming the first African American Field Service exchange student ever sent to Belgium."

Cadet is convinced that the resolve of minorities to succeed professionally is steeled by their encounters with racial discrimination. "We become very hardened and tough-minded as a result of our experiences. If you're Black it's simply not good enough for you to be good; you have to work twice as hard to counter the stereotypes that are accepted by many whites by default—like a computer on a default setting. Some of us simply have to be part of the 'reprogramming' process. So I'm appreciative of what I went through in the tenth grade because it prepared me for what I had to go through later in the business world."

Success in Politics—With Setbacks From Office Politics

Majoring in economics at Stanford University, Cadet got her feet wet in the economic development field as an aide to U.S.

Rep. Charles Diggs, then head of the House Subcommittee on Africa. After helping Diggs draft legislation to create the Sahelian Development Program, which provided long-term aid to the drought-stricken region, Diggs was so impressed with Cadet's economic acumen and political savvy that he put her in charge of the program, which she ran from 1973 to 1975 while completing her degree.

Diggs sent her to Africa "where I got a first hand view of developmental problems as they related to the land and the people: where the challenge was to help them put these scarce resources to work to develop their economy." The food assistance program was a resounding success, growing from a seed capital of $23 million to a $1 billion development program for West Africa and is still in existence today.

Anybody else would have parlayed these stellar credentials into a career in politics, either angling for a cabinet post in the nation's capitol or glad-handing for votes on the hustings. But not Cadet. Her first taste of politics left a bad taste in her mouth.

"I couldn't stomach the notion of positioning for different appointments, the gaining of temporary alliances and so on. On the other hand, I still wanted to be an effective player in the development field and I thought the best way to do that in my earlier career was government service."

Cadet used her food-aid background to secure a job with the California Department of Food and Agriculture, rising to the post of surplus food director for the state, where she oversaw the distribution of $254 million worth of surplus food to needy residents.

Unfortunately, Cadet found that you can't avoid office politics when you're working with civil servants who march in lockstep to the motto: "But we've always done it that way!"

"I'd constantly encounter a lot of resistance to my suggestions to improve the food distribution process. So I developed ways to effectively counter that attitude by being more well-researched in any given area. My secret? By networking with community service groups I'd come to the table with more information. The others in the department knew that I had done the research demonstrating my approach so ultimately their response was, 'Let's do it her way.' "

Cadet observes that, in general, women come to the conference table better armed to defend their strategy to solve a business problem precisely because they anticipate being challenged. "Women are more 'proactive' than men as an astute response to having been excluded from the old boy network."

Not only was Cadet able to nimbly scale hurdles to organize the state's distribution system but created a computer program that scheduled its distribution and successfully lobbied for $2 million in public financing for the department. However, while these accomplishments may have looked dazzling on her resume, they couldn't help her accomplish what mattered most: breaking into management.

After five years with the department, she asked to be considered for Deputy Director, an appointed position, and was passed over for the job in favor of a white male with a less-impressive track record. Her reward for a job well done was a patronizing pat on the head and *not* a promotion, a "benign" form of discrimination that all too often derails women from their career destinations. "The message that was implicitly conveyed to me was, 'We appreciate your services and if you stay on for a little longer perhaps we'll be able to promote you.' And the business about staying on for a little longer after I had already put in five years didn't suit me well."

Moving to the Private Sector—And Another Old-Boy Network

Cadet had decided it was high time to get out of government anyway and switch to the private sector lest she be earmarked a civil service drone. Her next move was to a transitional job in a quasigovernmental company. As director of a semiprivate management consulting firm that counseled minority- and female-owned small businesses on management, loan packaging, and market development, Cadet developed the management experience she needed to affect her entree into the private sector.

"As the advocate for a minority-owned new business, I learned a lot about loan packaging and selling new ideas to bankers. That gave me a foot out of government business and a foot into the corporate side."

It was after leaving that job in 1988 to take a position as director for state operations for an aerospace engineering firm that Cadet got her second exposure to the old-boy network. Unlike her stint in state government, this time she got the title she deserved. But she was saddled with a secretary so incompetent Cadet spent more time putting out her fires than carrying out her official job duties drumming up new business from state and local governments. What's worse, she reported to a management that was indifferent to her requests for a replacement and would instead tell her to "work around the problem."

"The secretary would constantly miss deadlines to pay bills as instructed or to submit proposals and consistently 'forget' where she filed things. I spent so much time correcting her work that I had very little time left to bring in new contracts. But when I brought in documentation of her sloppiness and examples of insubordination to my management, they kept telling me to 'work around it.'

Cadet put two and two together: If she couldn't replace an unproductive staff member, she couldn't do her own job and hence would be black-marked with a poor performance evaluation when review time came at the end of her first year on the job. It was time to look for a new job.

Cadet maintains that too many women don't realize that dead-end job situations don't always manifest themselves as blatant "no-you-can't" turndowns but rather as diversionary "maybe later" tactics.

"I suppose I could have waited a couple of years for management to replace the secretary but I wasn't willing to work under those conditions and I doubt they would ever have responded to me because the request was a low priority for them, coming from a woman. Interestingly enough, the man who filled my position was permitted to fire her shortly after he took the job."

She makes the same assessment of her predicament at the state agriculture department, where the climate for female advancement hasn't improved much since she left. As she puts it, "It's been ten years since I left and to my knowledge they still don't have any women in key jobs there." So if she'd taken her boss' advice to put in more time before vying for another promotion, she'd probably still be there—"doing time."

Gaining Recognition in a Smaller Firm

Fortunately, just as Cadet was preparing to bring her résumé up to date for circulation, a friend told her about a job opening with her current employer, River West Developments. In the space of a few months she was promoted to Vice President, responsible for capital budgeting and forecasting for land developments worth over $100 million.

At River West, where Cadet has worked since 1989, she says she has finally found a working environment where her talents are recognized. "I've only been at River West for 14 months and I've been promoted from Business Manager to the Vice-President—it's been that kind of environment. For those of us who believe in a meritocracy, the quest is to find a company that operates with that ethic. I just want to reassure other women that there are meritocracies out there."

Cadet advises other women who find loathsome the corporate rituals of fawning over higher ups whose star is in the ascendancy and icing out those who are on the outs—women who prefer to be judged on what they know and not whom they know—to consider working for a smaller firm.

"I discovered in the course of working for the aerospace company that the prospect of climbing the corporate ladder in a large company involves playing a lot more political hard ball than I really care to play. Sure, I could spend a lot of time in that environment learning how to play hard ball, affiliating myself with the appropriate mentors and the whole bit, but the tradeoffs weren't worth it. And the length of time it would take to get anywhere within the company isn't worth spending."

Who's on Top? Dealing with Resentful Male Subordinates

Like most of the other female executives profiled in this book, Cadet has had to contend with the fact that men aren't used to "having the woman on top." Most male subordinates don't defy a woman's authority outright but simply deny it by refusing to produce—which, in turn, sabotages the woman's ability to meet her business goals.

Cadet relates one such example: "I would need financial data from this man and his staff and it would come in very slowly or not at all. The individual would 'lose' invoices that we needed."

The man clearly resented performing what he considered clerical duties, and for a woman, at that! Cadet's solution was to relieve him of these "demeaning" tasks by assigning them instead to his secretary, which in effect resulted in a promotion for her since she became the "liaison" between her boss' department and Cadet's.

"I told him that as the liaison to our department, she would attend our meetings in lieu of him because he was so 'busy.' "

That administrative move solved the immediate problem: making sure the work got done. But Cadet also makes a practice of getting resentful subordinates to talk through their feelings to ensure that they don't undermine the long-term business relationship.

"I'll say, 'You know, John, we're not communicating like we used to. Could it be that you're resentful because I've gotten this new position?' I just come right out with it. Having done that, I can try to assure him that I'm still part of the team, even though I have different duties. I'll tell them that if they need my help progressing in their careers I'll be there for them and I'll pass on any information I might get because of contacts in my new position and new surroundings that could improve their job status or job security.

"At the same time, I'd encourage them 'to pass tidbits on to me and maybe we'll help each other to continue to climb this corporate ladder. Maybe you'll get promoted next year and I may need some of your favors,' that sort of thing.

"Using this approach lets them know that I am still their ally even if I'm not still their colleague—usually defuses the tension as long as I follow through on my commitments. Otherwise I would appear totally insincere and the resentment would grow even deeper."

Avoiding the Most Subservient Tasks: Making Coffee and Taking Notes

Rarely is a woman's self-esteem as a professional more threatened than during staff meetings, where male and female colleagues vie for approval for their ideas from a superior. In these discussions men will often attempt to gain the upper hand over the woman in the room by assigning her a subordinate clerical role at the meeting, ignoring her ideas, or pretending to ignore her ideas and then coopting them. Cadet has developed effective antidotes to these practices to ensure that she is neither treated like a secretary, nor as a corporate "ghostwriter."

"I purposefully sit away from the coffeepot, for example. So that if I'm asked to get coffee, I'll say: 'Would you please ask the gentleman at the other end of the table who is closer to the coffee pot to get the coffee?' I think that's the polite way, the diplomatic way of letting people know that you have the same status they do."

Cadet also makes it crystal clear that not only does she *not* "do windows" or get coffee but she doesn't take notes at the meeting either, unless it's by her choice. While many women are fearful of drawing attention to their elevated status by making a scene over being relegated to these duties lest they be earmarked as an ill-tempered feminist, Cadet's approach is always to give the erring male the benefit of the doubt.

"There are a zillion ways to politely deflect a pejorative request to take notes without drawing attention to your status in a hostile manner. If a woman who is truly an executive is asked to take notes, she simply needs to say, 'Sure, I can *provide* you with a note-taker, let me get my secretary.' The message is clearly conveyed: not only is she not a secretary, but she's attained sufficient rank to have one. Alternatively, you can simply say: 'I'd suggest you ask John (a man of equal rank to you) instead. He has better note-taking skills than I.' After a while they get the message and they won't ask you to do it."

In most cases, however, Cadet "does her research" before attending a meeting to preempt such encounters. "Before I go into a meeting I'll pop in to see if other men have brought notepads to take notes. If they haven't and if I'm in charge of the meeting I bring a secretary with me. If I'm not in charge of the meeting and it's male-dominated, I'll keep a note-pad hidden which I'll only pull out to jot down notes for my own edification."

Whether or not the note-taking role is a subservient one, however, depends on the context, Cadet says. For example, if you as a note taker wind up as the only participant with a permanent record of the proceedings, that information gives you power that others don't have.

"You gain control over the information disseminated. If I'm in charge of the notes, I have 'the scoop' on the information discussed at the meeting so it's now up to me to disseminate that information."

Making Sure Your Ideas Are Heard—And That *You* Get the Credit

It's one thing to keep a record of everybody else's thoughts and quite another to ensure that a woman's input is part of the minutes of the meeting under her "copyright." Cadet maintains that men often do worse than merely ignore a woman's contribution to a discussion—or dismiss it—they'll appear to discount the idea's importance and then reintroduce it into the discussion as their own idea!

"I combat the practice by dropping just a kernel of an idea in a meeting and withholding the rest. And, of course, the typical response to a female voice by the other participants is not to acknowledge the idea right away. Sooner or later a male in the room will restate the idea. Once that's done I'll "second the motion," complete the idea, and leave the other person in the dust. They didn't have the 'finishing pieces' to the idea because I intentionally withheld them."

One-on-one lunch meetings with a male colleague pose a slightly different challenge to a woman's authority: Instead of ignoring a woman's remarks outright, the man across the table may sabotage the goals of the meeting by dragging the conversation into the quicksand of small talk. Cadet takes charge of the agenda to ensure that business and pleasure don't mix.

"For example, on one occasion, when I wanted to discuss some office procedures with a man, I took a written agenda of the items I wanted discussed with me to the lunch table. I had an extra copy of the agenda but I never volunteered it to the gentleman so that I'd stay in control of the meeting. And I just made sure we went through all the issues before the entrees were served. Sure enough, he jotted down his commitments and we enjoyed a leisurely lunch."

After all, there's no harm in leaving time for small talk and catching up on office gossip, as long as it's the woman who is in charge of adjourning the regular meeting to discussion "other business."

Life in a Two Career Household— *Without* the 'Second Shift'

Like the other working mothers profiled in this book, Cadet never felt guilty about not staying home to raise her twin daughters. "As a child, I was always reassured by my Mom that it was my choice to work or to stay home and that I did not have to replicate her choice to stay home. For that reason, I just never had a guilt trip about working at the same time I'm raising my daughters, who are nine years old."

What's more, Cadet and her husband run an "equal opportunity" household; her husband does his share of household duties. This partnership also exists in the marriages of the other executive women profiled in this book, contradicting a 1989 University of California study entitled "The Second Shift" that maintains that even full-time working women do 75 percent of the housework.

"Both my husband and I have "second shifts"—we share in the household and child-rearing responsibilities. I'm married to a modern man. He's involved with the household: he does dishes, he cooks, shares child care responsibilities, does the homework assignments with the kids. Sure, there's a lot more that he could do, but he does so much compared to other men that I have no complaints."

Cadet recognizes, however, that two career families can't always have their cake and eat it: If both spouses have to travel extensively on business, quality time with the kids could suffer.

"One of the reasons I left my last job was the fact that travel was interfering with raising my kids. Now travel assignments would probably be less detrimental because my children are older; but at the crucial ages between four and seven they needed me to help them develop study habits." Neither could Cadet accept an international assignment to advance her career, since her husband would not have easily continued his law practice overseas. Since then his practice has included more overseas clients so the move wouldn't be as difficult.

"I had an offer to work at an international company at the same time I got the offer for my current position and I turned it down in favor of this job because this one is local. My husband simply couldn't drop his clients to join me abroad for just a year and half. What would he do when he came back? So I made a conscious choice to enrich my life on the 'family side' by taking a local job."

What To Do If You Don't Find a Mentor

Cadet says that throughout her career she's had to marshall her own emotional and intellectual resources in order to advance rather than look to an ally in the corporate hierarchy to teach her the ropes—or help her climb them. But that doesn't mean she doesn't value the importance of a mentor for other would-be female executives. Her solution: if she couldn't have one, she'd be one.

"How seriously do I take the concept of a mentor? Very seriously. And that's why I created the Sacramento chapter of the National Association for Female Executives, which has grown from two members when I started it exactly a year ago to more than four hundred members. One of the most important functions of the organization is a mentor program. I'm personally a mentor for about twenty of these women and I'm doing it because I didn't have one and could have used one through the years."

Cadet declares that the closest thing to a mentor she's had is her husband, who has served as a sounding board for her ideas and a sympathetic ear for her frustrations. "How crucial has my husband been for my career success? On a scale of one to ten, I'd give him a nine and a half. He has always backed up my decisions as well as come up with different strategies for me to test to enhance my performance or improve my relationships with subordinates."

Encouraging Yourself: "I'm Powerful and Strong"

Cadet says that because women so frequently have had to serve as their own cheering sections, she's developed a mental tonic that delivers a concentrated dose of encouragement whenever she's faced with a tough business challenge and plagued by self-doubts.

"I think we women professionals have to remind ourselves that we are indeed powerful, strong, and capable before exposing ourselves to any challenge, because in doing so we can transform the way that we consequently behave. Marcus Aurelius said it best in 300 A.D.: We become what our thoughts are.

"Have you ever tried stretching out your arm and saying, 'I'm powerful and I'm strong' ten times? And then ask someone to pull your outstretched arm down to your side? The person is not strong enough to do it, whether they're male or female, child or adult. But then ask them to try it after you've said instead, 'I'm weak and I'm unworthy' ten times. You can't keep the arm up.

"I find that saying those five words is the most empowering tool that I can use when facing not only my business challenges but my personal challenges as well. If you're faced with the challenge of entering the boardroom somewhat unprepared on your subject matter and your self-confidence is riddled by negative thoughts, such as 'Oh, no, these male chauvinists are going to challenge me,' you'll likely fail to achieve your objectives. But if you go into that same boardroom just as unprepared but steeped in the concept that you're powerful and strong, you'll transform the way that you handle any challenge."

chapter 10

Jacquie Arthur
of M/A-Com:

STAYING ON TRACK AFTER BEING DERAILED

Most executives of an acquired company can report losing sleep over whether they'll emerge as insiders with genuine power in the new regime or as exiles to corporate Siberia with fancy titles but no turf.

That was the dilemma Jacquie Arthur had to resolve in mid-October 1990 following the merger between her employer, Dennison Manufacturing Co. where she had been a Senior Vice President, and Pasadena, California-based Avery International Corporation. Unlike many executives in an acquired company who are ushered out with a golden parachute and a going-away party, Arthur was "permitted to stay on the plane" with the job offer of Vice-President of Strategic Operations. The unresolved question: Would the job put her on a path to the pilot's seat?

"Some people are clearly pushed out of the airplane; they've got their parachutes and they're pushed out. But that wasn't my situation. And you're never sure whether the only reason the company is keeping you on is because they've got to pay you anyway. So I had a number of concerns about what the job really was—it seemed to be something of a concocted job."

Her suspicions seemed to be vindicated. Several other of Dennison's officers who were similarly "kept on the plane" discovered that their jobs had more style than substance and left the company within a year, Arthur said.

But "takeover angst" carries a double whammy if you're a

woman executive under these turbulent circumstances, Arthur reports—an executive who also has to determine that her purpose in the new entity won't be a "let's-showcase-the-fact-we've-got-an-executive-woman" one.

"One of the little carrots that Avery Dennison's management held out to me was 'Maybe the job we're offering to you will allow you to get into operations and line management.' And I would ask, 'How?' But even after talking it over at length with the president of the company I wouldn't get a satisfactory answer."

Arthur had good reason to be skeptical about her prospects: Avery had no women in senior "line" positions, where an executive's function contributes to the company's bottom line. Their only female executives—the head of human resources and the head of communications—were in staff positions. "Companies tend to let women do the soft stuff, but God forbid they should run a factory." Why does line experience matter? In most companies it's a prerequisite for an officer's job.

Arthur ultimately made the tough decision to turn the job down, one which not everyone would have the courage to make since the job represented career security for her at a time when Massachusetts firms were retrenching and trimming staff.

"When you've got to make a career decision and you don't have another job waiting in the wings it's hard to say, 'I just don't think this is right for me.' It was a very difficult decision to make, extremely difficult. But as soon as I did it I started to feel better."

The Need for Line Experience to Break the Glass Ceiling

In December 1990, Arthur accepted an offer to join M/A-Com, Inc., a $375 million Burlington, Massachusetts-based defense contractor that makes microwave components, as its Vice-President and Treasurer.

She's comfortable with her choice, but she still has no iron-clad guarantees that she'll shatter the glass ceiling after all. Sure, her name is listed right under that of the Chairman and CEO in the company's annual report in the section entitled "executive officers." But that doesn't mean she's a heartbeat away from the CEO's job.

Arthur's dilemma, common to many within the elite corps of female executives in this country, is that not everybody in management considers her background in finance as credentials in the category of line experience. Arthur insists that executives who run their company's treasuries (as she does) make crucial decisions that have bottom-line impact.

"There's quite a bit of debate in financial circles about this, but in my mind, running the treasury is running a business: a business that's involved in money management. For much of the last 10 years I've had tax responsibility, and every tax dollar you save is a dollar that goes straight to the bottom line."

So Arthur's challenge is to work at a company whose management will either take her track record seriously or give her the management opportunities routinely afforded male executives who are considered fast-track material. Has she finally found that employer in M/A-Com? Only time will tell.

"Without line experience it's going to be impossible to be CEO at many companies. But what steps I take to get the experience really depends on how far I want to go with my career and in which type of company—because there are companies that do have a career path all the way to the top through the finance side.

"It's one of life's challenges, but I'm not sure how crucial it is to resolve it at this point in my career. My challenge at this stage is to get to the next rung on the ladder. It's like playing chess: I'm thinking several moves ahead and deliberating about which pieces I have to retain to win the game."

Destined for Success

Arthur has been thinking several moves ahead about her future since she was a child growing up in the United Kingdom, very likely because she is a product of a father who was hoping for a proactive Jack and not a passive Jacquie.

"I was living out the expectations of both a boy and a girl, which I think is significant. My father spent a lot of time reading to me and playing tennis with me when I was a child. I was in the boy role and he always took me very seriously. My mother always treated me as if I were going to be successful at something. So I think I had an advantage as an only child."

By the time she was 16 she had completed 11 college preparatory exams called 'O levels,' when even the most ambitious Oxford and Cambridge University-bound students typically take eight at the most. What's more, most of her exams were in the "tough subjects": science and math, since Arthur was prescient enough to realize that if she were going to succeed in business, a concentration in Elizabethan literature or Renaissance art simply would not cut the mustard.

Her first move on the chessboard was to get an education that would prepare her to succeed in a man's world. "I wanted to continue taking science and math at my school but it was designed to turn out nice young ladies who were interested in the arts. I decided pretty much independently that I wasn't getting the technical education that I needed, so I applied to a local technical college—what Americans would call a prep school. While the president of the college initially told me he didn't have enough room for me until the following year, he gave me a place immediately when I told him I had 11 O levels."

Arthur also benefited from the fact that there was a labor shortage in Great Britain in the late 1960s, so companies apparently became gender-blind in their search for top-notch students. British Petroleum snatched up Arthur in 1967 before she had even graduated high school, sponsoring her to study economics and engineering at City University in London.

Women Execs in the U.S. Versus the U.K.

Following her "internship," Arthur was recruited into BP's internal audit department, where she evaluated the performance of the company's large capital investments while qualifying as an accountant. Impressed with her insights and her spunk— Arthur would frequently debate conventional accounting wisdom with the company's grey eminences even though she was barely out of her teens—the senior economist recruited her into a think tank reporting to the board of directors. She studied such issues as the impact of oil shortages on overall energy supply. "This got me into a group that was very visible when I was still only in my mid-twenties."

At that point she met her mentor, then the director of finance for British Petroleum, who had helped set up BP's New York office. He was instrumental in sending her to New York as Vice-President of Finance for BP North America in 1982. "Going to the U.S. was seen as a development move for me—I was financially-oriented but I needed to understand the market in Europe and in the United States."

And unlike many married executive women whose two-career households would be disrupted by overseas assignments, Arthur has a husband with a "portable" profession. "Because my husband is an academic and a lot more flexible than many people in his career moves, he was able to come with me."

Moving to the United States not only turned out to be a very good career move, but it opened Arthur's eyes to a different business culture—one which she believes is a superior culture for female executives.

"I was doing business frequently with banks and found it easier to deal in the American and New York marketplace than in the European marketplace. I found the acceptance of senior women much greater here than in the U.K. So I really enjoyed it here."

Arthur also had a hunch that the acceptance of the idea of senior women having babies and returning to work was probably greater in the U.S. than in the U.K., if the maternity-leave policy of BP's London office was any barometer. The rule there: "When you show, you go."

"There was a requirement in the London office that women take their maternity leaves when they were seven months pregnant. As a result, the few women in that office who did have children—and there were very, very few—would systematically lie about their due date so that they could work as long as possible."

Arthur recalled the day in the mid-1980s when her boss called her in New York from London to tell her about a female colleague who had just given birth "two months prematurely."

"He told me, 'Now, I don't know much about these things,

but the baby weighed in at eight and a half pounds—a pretty good size.' He was basically telling me he knew what was going on."

If You Can't Move Up, Know When To Move On

Once her mentor retired after she had been in the U.S. for four years, Arthur decided to sever her ties with BP and the British corporate culture altogether and look for work at an American company.

"I wanted to be a more senior person in the management team rather than go back into something that was rather hierarchical and bureaucratic. And I wanted to be in the United States and in a smaller company. So it was a combination of reasons that made me want to join another company. I had been with BP for 19 years so it was very hard."

So when a headhunter told her about an opening for Vice-President and Treasurer at Dennison Manufacturing Co. in 1986, it seemed like a perfect fit: the company needed her expertise in finance and there appeared to be opportunities for advancement. "So I put it all together and decided that it was the right place to be."

Arthur adds that the chairman of the company was intrigued by the idea of having a woman. "I find that men with adult daughters who are working are much more ready to accept senior women. And the chairman had two daughters."

Arthur wasted no time in reorganizing Dennison's outmoded financial organization, revamping its treasury and consolidating the debt amassed by its worldwide subsidiaries. In 1989 she was rewarded for her efforts with a promotion to Senior Vice-President of Strategic Planning, where she oversaw planning and corporate development for the $800 million diversified manufacturer.

Encouraging Diversity in the Workplace

While she was pleased with her accomplishments at Dennison, she wasn't convinced that she had shattered the glass ceiling.

"I think that somehow I snuck in on top of it. And in fact Dennison probably had a 'glass sandwich' because I snuck in on top of a ceiling and there was one above me. While there were women in middle management jobs, there were no women line managers. And although we said we wanted senior women and we wanted women to advance, the company didn't seem to be able to make it happen."

Arthur was part of an effort to "bootstrap" the process as a member of a diversity committee Dennison had set up to get more women and minorities into management. "Along with creating a human resources function to develop lower- and middle-management women, we also set up a monitoring program biasing the selection process in favor of women and minorities." Avery International was impressed enough with the program that it hoped to continue it in its new identity as Avery-Dennison, Arthur said.

While Arthur acknowledges that there are barriers to women climbing up the management ladder in corporate America as well as corporate Europe, she also believes that many women self-impose these obstacles by setting their sights too low.

"I think one of the things that frustrates me the most when I try and help other women is their low perception of themselves. They almost put the glass ceiling over themselves. They say, 'I really would like to make it to head of marketing and sales' but when I suggest, 'Why not the General Manager?,' it's too much of a stretch."

Perhaps because many women have such low self-esteem, they have a tough time understanding that when it comes to motivating subordinates, the effort of the whole group is greater than the sum of its parts, Arthur says.

"I don't know why it's the case but most women have a hard time understanding the value of teams. I see women having a harder time delegating, motivating, valuing the contribution of a group of people. They say 'this person can do this and somebody can do that' but they don't see that if you add those parts together you might get more.

"And working in teams is so important if you're going to be in a senior position. I don't know where I developed my understanding of it, perhaps it was back in engineering school where all my friends were men. But somewhere along the way I recognized this."

How Corporate Culture Affects How Women Are Treated

It's one thing to be a woman who is comfortable with men's ways of managing and another to work with men who aren't comfortable with women. Arthur admits that while she may have had an easy time hanging out with the guys as an engineering undergraduate, she finds corporate culture to be stuck in the Dark Ages—or perhaps the age of chivalry—as far as relationships between men and women are concerned.

"There are some men who think that it's very strange to call a woman and say, 'Let's have lunch.' And I think it works the other way: Men would be very uncomfortable if women call and say, 'Let's have lunch.' It's very much an issue for me and, frankly, I don't know how to deal with it."

Even more frustrating than putting up with a dearth of lunchtime companions outside of the office—and thereby being cut off from a steady flow of useful office gossip—is convincing male colleagues to take her ideas seriously, even with Arthur's impeccable credentials and impressive title.

"I find that men don't necessarily register what a woman is saying but they'll register what a man says. However visible a woman is, they just ignore her. I think the only way that women can deal with it is to keep having ideas and to make sure they keep surfacing. And eventually the others will sort of default to you. But I think that's a very real problem."

The Benefit of Workforce Diversity: Women Have a Different Perspective

Arthur has observed that during those occasions when she insists on being heard by her male colleagues she has been able to offer a fresh perspective on the entrenched, we've-always-done-it-that-way, old-boy approach to management. She maintains that it's the advantage of having that perspective that should motivate management to take the ideas of the diverse workforce seriously.

"There are two reasons why people are interested in women getting to the top. One is pure demographics: The workforce of tomorrow is going to be diversified. If you ignore that, you're just being foolish.

"The other reason is that enlightened companies realize diversity brings a new approach to solving problems: As a woman I see things a different way. And sometimes I'm heard and sometimes I'm not, sometimes I'm right, and sometimes I'm not."

By illustration, Arthur talks about an occasion when she suggested—without saying so—to others in management that employees ought to be treated like members of a corporate family rather than like children.

"We had scheduled a shareholder's meeting while Dennison was going through the merger and quite a large number of the employee shareholders had asked to come to the meeting. Traditionally, the company would have a special meeting for them. When we discussed their request in a management committee meeting, the consensus was that it wasn't worth the effort to have them come to this meeting because it wasn't going to be anything special; we were simply going to take a vote.

"I disagreed. I said, 'I think it's very important that they come.' I said that the importance of the meeting wasn't what was being resolved but whether or not the employees could participate in it because it serves the same purpose for them as a funeral.

"And they all looked at me. And suddenly they realized what I was saying, that it really doesn't matter that it was a nonevent of a meeting, that for many of these employees the meeting represented a separation process from the company where they had worked for many years. In some cases they devoted their entire careers to it. And they had to go through a process of parting."

Arthur's view prevailed. "We opened the meeting up, and as it turned out relatively few turned out compared to what we expected. But my point is, I had a slant on this situation which was very different from everyone else's. And I have hundreds of stories like this, but that's this week's one. That's why I think that members of the diverse workforce are more likely to see things from a lot of different angles."

chapter 11

Linda Wroblewski
of Richard A. Eisner & Co.:
"SOMEDAY YOU'RE GOING TO BE PARTNER"

Even straight-A accounting graduates are supposed to put up with at least one mind-numbing arithmetic exercise on their first job fresh out of college. But to Linda Wroblewski, tallying the ballots for music awards as her first assignment at Laventhol & Horwath in 1978 amounted to the undeniable moral equivalent of clerical work.

After a couple of days of dutifully putting check marks in little boxes, Wroblewski decided that if the accounting firm were going to be paying her top dollar for her talents—$14,200 a year—it ought to be getting its money's worth.

She marched down to the Personnel Director's office and made him an offer. "I said I could get my brother who was 16 to come in here and do this, I can pay him half what you're paying me, keep the profit and do something else with the rest of my time. This assignment is not exactly challenging—I came here to learn."

So the next day her fellow new hires continued to tally ballots and Wroblewski was sent into the field to do an audit. Sometimes you have to come right out and ask for what you know you're worth even when there's not yet a "track record" to back you up.

Wroblewski not only knew her own worth but her superiors at the Manhattan office of the national accounting firm apparently sensed her potential as early as her first job interview.

"I was interviewed by the senior partner because the person who was supposed to talk to me was out sick. And this partner said to me, 'You know, one day you're going to be sitting in my chair. The only person that's going to stop you from getting to the top is yourself. If you want to do it and you have the talent and the business sense you're going to make it here.' "

Wroblewski had originally planned to build a career at one of the Big Eight firms and had only interviewed at Laventhol & Horwath to widen her field of choices. But that conversation with the senior partner stopped her dead in her tracks.

"As I sat there and listened to him I thought, 'Yeah, that's something I can do. That's something I want to do.' The firm was small enough that I thought one day I could run it. And that's why I made the decision to join it."

Learning to Think Quickly—And to Absorb Everything

Wroblewski's Polish emigre parents were concentration camp survivors who didn't prepare her so much for a career as they did for thinking on her feet. Which is literally what she had to do as a youngster when she made change for customers in their Brooklyn candy store.

"I didn't use the cash register, I had to add up everything in my mind—I didn't have time to write it down. I think my parents wanted me to work in order to sharpen my mind, so that I'd know what it was like to have a dollar, to think quickly. My parents' mindset was that there was one thing that no one could take away from you: your mind, your intelligence.

"But they didn't encourage me to be a professional. I always did very well in school because I liked it. I loved knowledge. I'd absorb everything I could, whether I was watching people or reading a book."

Once she entered the professional working world at Laventhol & Horwath, Wroblewski also absorbed everything she could about the accounting business.

"While others would leave the office at 6 P.M. I would typically stay until 9 and read everyone else's work—last year's work papers, technical books—whatever I could to make sure that I did a good job. And if I had a question or didn't understand the entire concept behind somebody else's work paper, I would go ask whomever had done that particular paper to review it with me. Taking initiatives like that make you stand out.

"You only get part of the picture if you only learn your segment of the job. But I wanted to know everything else out there so I could evaluate the client's financial position."

Wroblewski credits her father for instilling in her an insatiable thirst for knowledge, for figuring out a better way of doing things.

"My father—who is one of the smartest men I know—learned whatever he knew through experience, as opposed to strictly book learning. He taught me how to look at a problem and figure out a different way of solving it. Sometimes in a big corporate world everyone's so involved in their own detail that they forget about the big picture."

Wroblewski had so impressed one of the firm's clients with her ingenuity that its management tried to lure her away with a high position in finance before she had even been with Laventhol & Horwath for one year.

Wroblewski's superiors were flabbergasted. "One of the partners asked the client, 'Why are you offering this woman a job? She's at the lowest professional level in the firm. We have any number of people senior to her with more experience. And the client answered, 'Because this woman comes up with ideas and has instincts; she has a business sense.'

"The reason they respected me is that I wouldn't just complete the assignment, I would go to the management of the company and say, 'Did you ever think of trying this or that approach?' Some might say who was I at 20 years old to give this man suggestions?"

Broadening Her Experience to Increase Her Marketability

After Wroblewski had worked the required two years to get certified as a CPA in 1980, she applied to law school to continue the education she felt was necessary to sharpen her acumen in the business world.

"I wanted the law degree and the legal knowledge because I think it makes you more well-rounded. For example, when we contemplate a merger or an acquisition I have the advantage of being able to see the entire picture."

But when she informed one of the managing partners that she was leaving the firm to go to school, he told her he had different plans for her.

"He said, 'No you're not. You didn't come from a family that has all these business contacts. I want you to stay and be my partner one day.' "

The upshot was that Wroblewski attended law school during the day and performed audits for the firm at night; an arrangement that she says was unprecedented in the firm's 66-year history. Despite the grueling schedule, she graduated near the top of her Brooklyn Law School class in 1983.

Her original intent was to leave the accounting firm and join a law firm: "I always did want to be like Perry Mason."

"After I interviewed at various law firms and got job offers, I came back to give notice to the senior partner I first interviewed with in 1978. I told him, 'You've all been great to me but I'm going to a law firm.' "

Again, the managing partners would not take no for an answer. But this time the senior partner must have realized he'd have to offer a pretty tempting carrot to keep Wroblewski away from the world of legal briefs, court dates, and closing arguments.

"He asked me, 'If you had your choice to do whatever you wanted, what would you want to do?'

Wroblewski thought back to her parent's Brooklyn candy store and the way they bootstrapped their way to financial security through sheer ingenuity and hard work. She figured that helping other such companies would be one way of paying them back. "I told him, 'I would really like to help small companies grow. That's what I'd really love to do.'

"He said, 'That's what you're going to do. You're going to build a department.' "

So at the tender age of 25, Wroblewski was handed the daunting assignment of building the Accounting and Business Advisory Services Department from scratch. The department grew to a staff of 25 who would assist some 200 businesses with their financial and business needs: from audits and tax returns to mergers, acquisitions, and estate planning. Sitting in an office that was twice the size of her parents' candy store, she and her department brought more than $1.5 million of business to the firm.

Not surprisingly, "growing" a start-up operation is not a pastime that most people like to pursue, since the likelihood of failure, and being associated with that failure, is so high. But Wroblewski doesn't believe in failure and she recommends that women make lemonade out of "lemon" assignments.

"The partners had previously asked selected partners and managers to start a similar type of department and everyone said no—I think I was their last choice. Did I take it personally that the other people turned the job down? Absolutely not. As far as I was concerned, it was their loss that they didn't realize this great opportunity. They did not have the foresight to see that small- and medium-sized businesses are major growth opportunities."

Gaining the Cooperation of Hostile Colleagues

Recognizing that as a 25-year-old neophyte Wroblewski needed to be brought up to speed in small-business matters, the firm's partners hired a consultant who was both a CPA and a lawyer to give her a two-year course in management.

However, far from sharing management's view of her as a quick study who would thrive under his tutelage, Wroblewski said the consultant regarded her contemptuously as a inconsequential little girl who by rights should be working for him. His hostile attitude was palpable at the department's very first meeting.

"The first thing he said to me in the meeting in this condescending tone of voice was, 'Do you have a written agenda that the rest of us can overview?'

Wroblewski felt no qualms about putting a man with an attitude problem in his place, even if the man were old enough to be her father.

"I turned to him and retorted something like, 'Is there some concept you would like to contribute?' There was silence in the room and I said, 'We will now continue.' "

"I'm convinced that he believed that he would take over the department and I would report to him. He was no doubt thinking, 'Who is this little girl? I know who I am. I know what I'm going to do.' "

During the next six months, Wroblewski says, the man did not consult her or her staff in the course of working on his assignment.

"He thought that he could do everything himself because he was the one with all this knowledge and experience. He didn't even think about finding out who and what I am and how we could help each other. Because he took that approach, he couldn't finish his assignment. As a matter of fact, at the end of the six months the firm's management was thinking of letting him go."

Wroblewski decided to give the man a last chance to work with her rather than against her—and at the same time give him an opportunity to save his own hide. She called him into her office, knowing that the deadline to hand in the project was looming and she had the ace in the hole: She and her staff had done his work.

"I told him, 'Listen, I tried to explain to you that this is my ball field and if you want to play you play by my rules. However, I'm going to give you an opportunity: I'm sitting here with the finished product. How do you want to play it? It's your call.' "

There was a moment of silence and then a shame-faced reply. "He told me, 'I now understand. I made a mistake.' "

"And I said, 'You're right, you underestimated me.' And we both started laughing and I gave him the package."

By holding her ground and insisting on her authority, Wroblewski says she not only won the man's respect but earned his friendship. "He has probably been one of my best friends and mentors over the years, he's been incredible."

Being Treated as an Equal

Wroblewski is not the sort of woman who worries if others don't take her ideas seriously, since she knows that the proof of an idea is in the outcome of its application.

"For example, my strategy for running my department was different than that of the other partners. The told me, 'We'll use a combination of your idea and ours,' and I assured them, 'Sure, we'll work it out.' I knew what I was going to do. And I figured as long as they're going to allow me to run the department I could do whatever I wanted to as long as I made a success of it."

Like other executive women, Wroblewski has had to deal with men who try to mask their jealousy of her career success in sarcastic put-downs. She simply smiles sweetly and lobs the sarcastic remarks right back over the net.

"A group of us were talking about how much business we brought in. After I spoke about my latest success in generating business one partner turns to another guy and says snidely, 'Well, it's her legs.'

"So I stuck out my leg and turned my ankle back and forth and replied, 'You know, you're right,' they are nice.' "

One of the partners at the firm once made the tactical error of asking Wroblewski, who was then a manager, to come into his office to "take a memo."

"My reply: 'Sure, I'd be happy to—as long as you type the memo up for me.' And he said, 'Maybe we should call my secretary.' I answered, 'What a good idea!' "

Don't Beat Around the Bush

"I think it's good to confront people if there's a problem. I don't believe in talking behind people's backs. If you're going to ask me a question you're going to get a true answer, a heartfelt answer. If you don't want to hear the truth, don't ask me, ask someone else. I don't believe in hemming and hawing."

Nor does Wroblewski have much patience with individuals who play politics by using their authority as a cudgel to intimidate her instead of working out a mutually agreeable solution.

"For example, a partner on the management committee in the New York office of Laventhol & Horwath once told me that one of the other partners whom I worked with on tax matters was unhappy about the way I was handling a client. He told me that the three of us would have to have a meeting to discuss the problem.

"I told the man, 'For one thing, the client's giving me plenty of business, so I don't see any problem. For another, if he's unhappy, he can tell me. The three of us are not going to meet, I'm going to handle it and I'll let you know the result.'

"I called up this other partner and I said, 'In the future if there's a concern that involves me you should tell me directly.'

His response was he didn't think I was involving him enough on this particular job, that I was ignoring him.

"I said, 'I can't call you up every five minutes and tell you what's happening. But if you would take the initiative and call me up I would be more than happy to give you a progress report.' "

"Someday You're Going to Make Partner"

In 1989, at the age of 31 Wroblewski became the first woman to make partner in the firm's New York office. She says she subsequently fielded scores of phone calls from women in other Laventhol & Horwath offices across the country asking for advice on how to make partner.

"My advice to other women is, don't let anything stand in your way. Don't allow things to happen to you, make them happen. Maybe that's the concentration camp mentality instilled by my parents."

Wroblewski proved that adage to herself when Laventhol & Horwath, the seventh largest accounting firm in the United States, filed for protection from creditors under Chapter 11 of the U.S. Bankruptcy code on November 21, 1990, handing out pink slips to its 3,500 employees in 51 offices.

Wroblewski not only landed on her feet after that setback (despite competing for jobs with 45 similarly unemployed former partners in Laventhol & Horwath's Manhattan office), but she landed on top again one month later, this time as a partner at a smaller, regional accounting firm, Richard A. Eisner & Co.

"As I was told when I first interviewed with Laventhol & Horwath in 1978, the only person who's going to stop you from getting to the top is yourself."

chapter 12

Sara Levinson
of MTV:

JUST DON'T ASK HER TO TYPE

MTV Vice-President Sara Levinson comes off so mellow and laid back you'd think she was a veejay on one of her programs, not a Columbia MBA who negotiates multimillion dollar licensing deals.

Her path to the top was nothing if not circuitous. During her college years she switched majors virtually every semester— from math to French to psychology to "human ecology." She spent more time marching for civil rights than hitting the books. For the first two years after graduation she bounced from one secretarial job to the next.

As Levinson, a Virginia native, puts it, "Sometimes I look back at the choices I've made and think: Boy am I one lucky individual."

Lucky? Maybe. More likely the influence of her mother, Esther, acted as a compass, steering her in the right direction but leaving it up to her how she achieved her goals.

"One of my brothers is a lawyer and as a child I can just remember my mother saying that she could envision a shingle outside the office that said Levinson and Levinson, with me being the other Levinson. She provided a lot of positive reinforcement to the notion of me taking care of myself, that I wouldn't get married until I knew who I was and what I was all about."

Levinson's mother once gave a prospective beau's father a

polite dressing-down for even suggesting that anybody but Sara would take care of Sara.

"I was dating a rather wealthy English person and the father of the guy was expecting my mother to be very excited to think that her daughter would be well taken care of by a wealthy family.

"He said to my mother, 'Sara will want for nothing.' And she replied, 'Sara will want for nothing on her own.' She just expected me to take care of business."

Levinson's mom, a history teacher, would have been a tough act to follow by anybody's measure.

"She dropped out of college in her junior year even though she was only one of two women at the time to be accepted to George Washington University Medical School. Instead she got married, waited until her youngest of five children was in kindergarten and went back and finished college with honors, then went on to graduate school with honors again, and wound up with a Fullbright fellowship to India."

Not only was Levinson's mom ahead of her time, to a certain extent she was ahead of her own daughter's generation.

"When I went to college between '68 and '72, the women's liberation movement hadn't really taken hold yet. My sister, who is four years older than I am, had gotten married right out of college."

Levinson's parents entreated her to enjoy herself at college and she took them at their word—during a period in history when virtually every student's studies were taking a back seat to political activism.

"I started out at Emory University in Atlanta and got involved in the whole anti-Vietnam War thing and in the civil rights movement, marching with Ralph Abernathy and the crowd. I was taking part in everything else but my studies."

Levinson transferred to Cornell University after two years. To save her parents money, "I wound up at the school of human ecology, which was the same thing as home ec. I was not focused, I was not directed. I wound up studying child development, behavioral psychology stuff. But not education; my mother refused to pay for any education courses. She did not want me to go into any typical female field."

After she received her bachelor's degree in 1972, Levinson worked in England for several months as a governess, long enough to decide that child development was not a suitable career: "At that point in my life the welfare of children definitely should not have been in my hands," she says drily. She moved to New York to live with her former college roommate who had gone to work for Chase Manhattan.

Climbing Out of the Typing Pool

It was in the Big Apple that Levinson discovered that her "unfocused" liberal arts degree was about as useful as a subway token in the desert. For two years Levinson bounced from one secretarial job to the next, first at the Institute of International Education then at similar kinds of jobs for *Harpers* magazine and in the ad sales department of the *Atlantic Monthly.*

Levinson reached the conclusion that if she were ever to climb out of the typing pool and 'take care of business' as her Mom decreed, she was going to have to get a master's degree in it.

"I really didn't want to go on to graduate school but at every job interview I would be asked how fast I could type. And I was the worst typist that ever walked the earth."

Levinson also looked to two other female role models besides her mother to keep her career track on the straight and narrow.

"My boss at the International Institute was the first woman to get a Ph.D. in business from the City College of New York. I thought, well, if this woman could do it, I could do something with my life. And my roommate was one of these women who knew what she wanted every step of the way. Even straight out of college with no MBA she had a résumé that looked like she'd been working for 30 years. She was offered tons of jobs and was put through Chase Manhattan's management training program and wound up earning $18,000 a year. And here I am a secretary and making $6,000!"

Unfortunately, even when Levinson was admitted to the elite corps of female MBAs in 1976, she found out that some people still believed that even women with white-collar educations are only entitled to pink-collar jobs.

"I remember I was so excited to get an interview at Warner Communications and got to talk to the president himself. He spent an enormous amount of time with me and then called the personnel department and told them to talk to me. And I thought, 'Wow, this is it, I'm going to be working for Warner!' "

Her elation was short-lived. "I went down to Personnel and would you believe the personnel director asked me how fast I could type! I thought, 'Oh my God, don't tell me I got the MBA for nothing after all, that I spent all this time and now I'm going to be going back to typing!' I volunteered to this woman that I could type for myself—I can't believe I even said that—but that was it. I just left there with a bad feeling."

Levinson theorizes that the personnel staffer reacted the way she did because women MBAs in 1976 were still as rare as women executives.

"There were very few women who had gotten MBAs at the time I got mine, although I think we had a higher percentage of women MBAs at Columbia than elsewhere. It was some time after that that huge numbers of women started getting MBAs."

Being in the Right Place at the Right Time—With the Right Skills

Levinson finally did land a job as an account executive at a company that took her degree seriously: at the ad agency Doyle, Dane and Bernbach, "a great first job to get straight out of business school." The agency put her on a fast-track training program for business school graduates along with three males.

"I was the first woman my boss had ever had working for him on any of his accounts and he told me he didn't know why he waited so long. He had a great sense of humor and I approach almost everything in my life with a sense of humor. We had a lot of fun."

Levinson left the company in 1978 to join Viacom International Inc., a $1.4 billion communications company that operates pay TV services, cable TV channels, and other interests, to work for its Showtime channel. Because while she loved her boss at DDB, she was getting bored with the work.

"After having worked on a couple of accounts at the agency for a couple of years I started seeing a repetition in the kind of work I was doing: package goods marketing. It just didn't stimulate me. And a huge opportunity came along as a fluke: Someone at the agency told me about someone they used to work for who was now at this new company called Viacom.

"So my motivation was not, 'Gee I want to work for the cable business,' or even 'I'm sick of advertising' but 'Gee, this is getting kind of boring and redundant and why not?' "

As Levinson puts it in her trademark self-deprecating style, "I was young enough to be able to afford to make stupid decisions for all the wrong reasons which turned out to be great ones: It got me in on the ground floor of an emerging industry. So I can chalk it up to being in the right place at the right time with the right skills."

Levinson blossomed in the start-up environment, rising rapidly to Manager of Advertising and Promotion, then to Director of Marketing for its cable division. She loved her job but in 1981 Viacom's management began discussing moving the cable division to San Francisco "and I was not interested in moving to San Francisco."

So she left the company to work for another broadcaster as a Marketing Group Vice-President of a start-up satellite operation. But while the job was challenging, a personality conflict with her boss unrelated to gender problems made it impossible for her to do her work. "It was the most miserable time I ever had in my life."

Once she started interviewing for another job she learned first-hand that women who act like victims of their circumstances not only don't go far on the job but won't have an easy time finding a new job, either.

"Whenever I'd go on an interview and people would ask me how my job was I'd tell them how miserable I was where I was working. And you just don't get a job doing that."

Fortunately, opportunity knocked on her door in 1984, as it had in 1978. Levinson had made enough of an impression on Viacom's management in her marketing and advertising jobs that she was lured back as Director of Corporate Development.

"I got a call out of the blue one day and this guy from Viacom says, 'We're looking for someone to head up corporate development and your name keeps coming up. You're seen as being bright and mature.' They had to choose between me and somebody else—a guy—and I was seen as much more mature."

Rising quickly through the ranks, in 1987 she was promoted to head of new business development for MTV Networks, where she pursued a host of products and spin-off businesses from the existing channels.

Her credits include creating an MTV record club, a Nickelodeon production studio, and a Spanish language program called MTV International which is aired throughout Latin America. Many industry observers credit her with finding new markets for an organization that was stuck in neutral during the mid-1980s, concerned chiefly with programming.

She describes her mission as "reaching our audience in other ways besides cable programming since these channels are extremely powerful trademarks—MTV and Nickelodeon in particular. They mean something to their audience in a way the Disney name does. So my job was writing the blueprint for these new business areas: from a financial level, from a strategic level, from a marketing level."

Levinson had wowed Viacom's management sufficiently with her knack at getting MTV Networks into the ring as a global contender that when the network's president resigned in 1991 to pursue other interests, she was named Executive Vice-President of Business Operations, where she splits the job of running the station with another woman, Judy McGrath. While Creative Director McGrath handles promotion, programming, and production, Levinson is in charge of the "business end" of the station: marketing, press, international, and new business.

Sadly enough, Levinson's Mom, Esther Levinson, died in 1982 before she could see her daughter take her place among the half a dozen top female executives in the cable industry, but not before she saw her get on the right track.

"She was at least able to see where I was headed, if not where I ended up. As far as she was concerned, where I was in 1982 was very much on an upward track. Mom was very supportive—she took a lot of pleasure in my accomplishments. I would say she lived her career vicariously through me."

Broadcasting Is Ideal for "Broads"

Even as a high-powered executive in a high-profile industry, Levinson shrugs off her success. She told a magazine reporter she was afraid to attend her 20th high school reunion in 1989 because "I thought everyone would feel sorry for me at the time because I wasn't married and didn't have a child."[51]

She's thrilled and gratified that other people think she's worthy of success.

"When I had been at Doyle Dane for six months and they gave me a raise to show me that I was doing a great job I said, 'Wow, this is neat. What did I do to deserve this?' Because success is all about being in the right place or taking a chance with a job and finding success."

Levinson says it was only recently that she started thinking "I am really destined for this stuff, I am doing a great job and they're goddam lucky to have me in this job."

On the other hand, she acknowledges she may have been fortunate enough to avoid confronting sex discrimination on the job simply because the broadcasting industry, particularly the cable segment, is more broadminded than others.

"At least in the communications business, I think there is a better environment for women. Just looking at MTV: the president of Nickelodeon, Geraldine Laybourne, is a woman and the MTV network's chairman has three senior women reporting to him."

Along with Levinson, Laybourne, and Judy McGrath, who is cohead of MTV, other standout women executives in the cable industry include Kay Koplovitz, President of USA Network, and Ruth Otte, President of the Discovery Channel and the Learning Channel.

Levinson says that there's a relaxed convivial atmosphere in her office where teasing and banter are the rule, not sexual tension.

"It's an open environment where women can say anything they want. When we have our staff meetings it's very much a humorous kind of atmosphere: If I'm not in the meeting or if one of the other women isn't there one of us will joke about how she can't handle it because, 'You guys are going to gang up on us.' If I'm the only woman in the room and I leave I'll come right back in the room and say: 'Now I know you guys are going to be talking about me when I'm gone.' "

Levinson says that one of the reasons why she's been successful in what still is predominantly a man's world, is that she doesn't walk around with a chip on her shoulder, conveying the attitude that the world owes her a living—or even a favor.

"I never threw it up in my bosses' face that I'm a woman.

And I think that's why they were happy to have me work for them: They took me under their wing, they taught me what they knew. They really wanted me to grow.

"When I hear younger women at my company blaming their frustrations on the 'male network,' the advice I give them is that the minute you start acting like a victim you become one. Basically, I believe that throwing the brick through the window the way we used to do in the 1960s is not the way you shatter the glass ceiling."

chapter *13*

Phyllis Swersky
of AICorp, Inc.:

SO MUCH FOR "THE MOMMY TRACK"

Phyllis Swersky always wanted to be the best, or at least have the best, as a child. She wasn't clear whether she'd accomplish her goals by making money or marrying into it.

"My aspiration even after graduate school was to sit by the pool at the country club," said Swersky, the Executive Vice-President and Chief Financial Officer of AICorp, Inc., a software developer. "During summers my biggest aspiration was how dark a tan I could get. And I remember the summer I went to work in my first full-time job my father bought me a sunlamp."

On the other hand, both Swersky's parents brought her up to be an achiever.

"I was very competitive and very achievement-oriented throughout school. A lot of that drive came from my mother; she wanted me to be the best, whether it was the best in class or the best-dressed. I was always number *three* at most; it always bothered me."

At the same time, "My father, an accountant, always told my sister and me that if you tried hard enough you could do anything. My father thought it was very important that I be self-sufficient. What if something happened to your husband? You needed to be able to take care of yourself. So that grounding is one of the roots of what I ultimately became.

"I think I'm also basically happier and don't tend to get as depressed as most people do. The reason for that is that my achievement motivation and competitive outlook were channeled in a constructive way. If I didn't work I'd be wondering who had the biggest house or the nicest car or the biggest diamond ring."

Choosing a Career That Offered Financial Rewards

So knowing that she had to support herself, the next challenge was finding a job that would support her in style. "My mother would always talk about teaching; it was such a nice profession for a woman. But teaching never really appealed to me—plus I figured for the same hours of working, why shouldn't I be able to earn a lot more money? Rather than a lot less money."

Swersky majored in sociology at Simmons College in Boston and by the time her junior year rolled around she realized that she didn't relish examining the origins of human behavior any more than she would have enjoyed grading papers.

"I thought, what am I going to do? Become a sociologist? That meant I would have to go on to graduate school and get a doctorate. And that just didn't appeal to me. The doctorate and then the academic life."

It was her dad who encouraged her to try accounting; she was familiar with the work because she had helped him do basic bookkeeping as a child. So after her junior year, she took an accounting course and was sold on the profession.

"And then I proceeded to go around to the then-Big Eight accounting firms and asked them how as a liberal arts major I could prepare myself to be hired by them. That's how I found out about a program sponsored by the accounting firms at Northeastern University called the Graduate School of Professional Accounting which gave Master's degrees in accounting to liberal arts graduates.

Once she entered the program, for the first time in Swersky's life she had a tough time making the grade, much less ending up at the top of her class. "I had never really worked hard before in my whole life; I coasted through high school, I coasted through college. It was never demanding or challenging. And this was overwhelming."

Swersky would rise at the crack of dawn to study, attend classes from 8 A.M. to 2 P.M., and collapse into bed to catch an hour or two's worth of sleep to compensate for having hit the books until 3 o'clock in the morning. "And do it all over again the next day."

The program was "the toughest thing I'd ever done. It was just like all the stories you hear about the first year of medical school and law school in which the school immerses you in your work because they're looking to get rid of those who can't cut it."

She would have dropped out but she didn't want to disappoint her father. "Not that he was pressuring me to stay, but I felt that I owed it to him. Here my parents were spending a fortune on graduate school after having already put me through college. "And I couldn't just turn my back on this. My father was incredibly proud of how I stuck at it and did well. Plus the experience was making me feel like I could do anything."

Getting Ahead by Making Career and Life Decisions

Swersky had "co-oped"—taken a program that enables students to combine study and work—at Coopers and Lybrand accounting firm, and the company asked her to join permanently upon completion of her Master's. "The Big Eight is just a fabulous way to enter the financial area. There's no better training ground."

However, Swersky left in 1976 after the two-and-a-half-year certification period because she couldn't take the pressure cooker environment, where back-to-back weekend work "made any kind of personal life impossible. I was constantly rushing to get home, to get to sleep so I could get up early so I could rush back to work. It was no way to live. So I decided to try industry."

She went to work for American Garden Products as Assistant Controller where she stayed until 1978 when the company was acquired. She left for Cullinet Software, where in eight years she rose to Senior Vice-President and Chief Financial Officer.

My career started to take off as the company grew. I became very career-committed. It was probably at that job that I sat back and said, 'I really like working, I'd like to see if I could get ahead.' And that's the way it happened."

Swersky left Cullinet in 1986 after the company founder brought in a new management team. She followed the former Cullinet president to AICorp. Among other accomplishments, she has played a key role in AICorp's international strategy, negotiating a sophisticated financing deal that enabled the company to introduce its advanced computer software throughout Europe.

"What's *She* Doing Here?"—When Clients or Colleagues Don't Take You Seriously

"The biggest problem I've had throughout my career is not being taken seriously. I experienced this the most frequently when I was the Chief Financial Officer of Cullinet and one of my major roles was presenting the company's stock to Wall Street investors. If I were to come to a meeting of portfolio managers and securities analysts they'd look at me as if to say, 'What's she doing here?' "

The solution, Swersky said, is simply to wow them with your competence. "I would always try to exude an air of confidence and being in control. And then it's strictly a question of responding with substance. When they start firing questions at you and you have the answer, they say, 'Hmmmmmm. She *does* know what she's talking about.' "

She also had to earn her right to be taken seriously by Cullinet's founder and chairman. "While I think he initially believed that a woman's place is in the home, as he watched the contribution I made and assessed my ability he came around. Women typically have to be better than men at their work. That's a fact. If there's any kind of resistance to a woman being a successful senior level executive you have to be better than the next man in your job. You've got to act the role before you have it—think strategically before it's your job to think that way. It's also the content of your ideas: having the answers and providing value to your superiors."

But on the whole, AICorp provides a work environment friendly to women, perhaps because as a software firm in a growth industry its employees tend to be younger and more entrepreneurial than they would be in an old-line manufacturing environment. "The whole attitude here is, let's find the best person to do the job. And hire outstanding people; it doesn't matter if they are male or female or Black or white or anything else."

A Mother's Place Is on the Job

For many working mothers the toughest challenge is proving they can mix motherhood with careerhood, since the common perception even today is that women are somehow defying nature when they hire somebody else to handle the 9-to-5 or 9-to-9 parenting shift.

Swersky, the mother of two boys and a girl in elementary school, says establishing that a mother's place is on the job is easier the second or third time around.

"My big concern with my first child—my daughter, who is now nine—was dispelling the perception among my coworkers that a mother's place is in the home. I adopted my daughter on a Wednesday and I was back to work the following Monday. Then when I adopted my son, who just turned seven, I said to myself, Now that I've got two kids to cope with I'll need to make an adjustment. And I've already proved that a mother's place isn't necessarily in the home. So I can afford to take a little more time off."

But while Swersky may have been out of sight of the folks back in the office during her leave, she wasn't out of their thoughts. "I left myself totally accessible: I was on the phone, I was doing a lot of work at home. And quite honestly, after three weeks of having one foot in the office and one foot at home, I said to myself, this is ridiculous; I'm going to feel a whole lot better and a whole lot more relaxed if I just go back to work. So I did."

Having done her part to demonstrate that women can be parents and productive workers simultaneously, she bristles at the notion that companies ought to accommodate the women who can't do both with a slower-paced "mommy track" to the top.

"I hate this mommy track concept and I'm dead set against it. I used to be against job-sharing and part-time work for women as well because I felt that the company got gypped and a lot of times the woman did, too. Why? Because in a high-tech environment we don't count hours; nobody's working a 40-hour week. If the company says we're going to job-share, is half time 20 hours? Baloney. A typical workweek is 50 or 55 hours. So with job-sharing either the company is getting shortchanged or the woman who gets paid by the hour is getting shortchanged.

"Where I have bottom-lined on the so-called mommy track issue is that it's not necessarily a male or female one. More and more men are saying to their employers: 'No, I don't want that job, it's too much travel and I have young children. I'm going to leave the company if you don't find another position for me.' And I've also modified my position on the issue of job sharing because there are certain people in the workforce who balance their work and personal lives in different ways than others— people who also add value to the company. So if you don't have these options available you lose valuable people."

There is certainly no "mommy track" in Swersky's suburban Massachusetts household. While Swersky earns enough money to afford a live-in nanny and housekeeper to fill in the gaps during her 10- and 11-hour workdays, that doesn't leave her husband, a CPA with his own practice, off the hook.

When Swersky's children were smaller she and her husband enrolled them in a cooperative nursery "so that both of us could be involved with our kids' school. We alternate parent responsibilities.

"The duties of raising our children are shared, there's a division of labor. I'm more in charge of organizing and setting their schedules. My husband probably spends more quantity time with them. He loves to play with them."

The Best Way to Change Things Is From Within: Evaluating the Climate for Change

While Swersky maintains that affirmative action measures were vital to getting women into the workplace, she believes that the changing demographics of the workplace will have a much more dramatic effect in helping them to get ahead than will any federal edict.

"The only way that a 60-year-old or 70-year-old man who has always viewed women with one stereotype will change is when his daughter cries bitterly to him after she was passed over for promotion." But Swersky observes that a significant chunk of the 30- and 40-year-old males have a different attitude about working women—based on the fact that many of them happen to be married to one.

Swersky provided an example of how the traditional male-female roles were changing within her company by showing how they're being transformed in the home. "I had a message handed to me recently from the male Vice-President of Finance who reports to me that said, 'Kids sick. Priscilla out of town. Home with kids.'

"Now, you can't get a more dramatic role reversal than that! And it's the existence of men like that one and their working wives that is going to effect change without the bitter fighting and clawing and EEO-style action.

"While the EEO has been successful getting women in the door, an EEO-style action will never get a woman on a company board. On balance, the best way to change things is from within. For example, when a woman recently resigned from our board of directors I told the chairman we had to find another woman to replace her. And he said, 'Okay, find me one.' So I'm the person who is in the best position to affect the glass ceiling in this company."

chapter 14

Carlene Ellis
of Intel Corporation:
"I DON'T BUY THIS WOMAN-AS-VICTIM BULL"

If you want to get Carlene Ellis' dander up, try to suggest that women have separate-but-equal abilities that should be accommodated in the workplace.

Ellis, a Vice-President at Intel Corp., earned her stripes as a business leader the hard way—learning discipline as a youngster by practicing ballet until her legs ached, practicing teamwork in high school by playing team sports, majoring in math and statistics in college—"the tough subjects."

To put it in her words, "I don't buy this woman-as-victim bull."

For that reason, Ellis doesn't see eye-to-eye with so-called experts on working women such as Felice Schwartz, who generated a furor in 1989 when she recommended that women who wanted to mix careers and motherhood be put on a slower track; the "mommy" track, as Schwartz' detractors derisively term it.

Says Ellis: "Felice Schwartz and I don't always see eye-to-eye, although I think she is trying to help women. I think that if the mommy track issue was misunderstood, as she says, she needed to set the record straight once and for all."

So when Schwartz approached Intel about doing consulting work for the company on so-called working mother issues, Ellis made sure she determined the agenda.

"We are considering doing a joint study with her on dual-career parenting, which really amounts to solving Intel's problem that we need very technically good people. A lot of those people happen to be female and Oriental, and how do I keep these women here once they want to have children?"

Unfortunately, these women don't necessarily have the same attitude about being a working mother that Ellis does—which is that it's perfectly okay to go back to work after giving birth and pay somebody else to take care of your kids. "Everybody's not like me and everybody doesn't want to do it that way. So that to me is the sixty-four thousand-dollar question."

Intel faces a manpower (or more accurately "woman power") crisis because a lot of the top-notch electrical engineering graduates from local colleges are Oriental women, who are torn between their high-tech minds and low-expectation cultures.

"While I don't have the data to prove it, I think we lose Asian women over cultural guilt. Often when they decide to have kids their mother gets to them and their grandmother gets to them and at that point they decide they can't do both. That's a great loss for our industry."

At the same time, the American kids, the ones who *do* come from a culture that says it's okay for moms to work, aren't mastering the technical subjects in school such as advanced math and science that would prepare them for an engineering career at Intel.

That wasn't the case with American kids growing up in the 1950s and 1960s.

Ellis and her older brother, who graduated from the Air Force Academy, were among the first in their extended family to go to college. Growing up in Jacksonville, Florida, 90 miles from what was then Cape Canaveral, their imaginations were ignited by the space program.

"We were products of the space era and the Sputnik scare and both of us (he ended up majoring in electrical engineering and I majored in math and statistics) pursued our education out of that urge to do something great. We thought that was the way to do it." But that was then and this is now.

"I don't know whether it's a California phenomenon or if it's happening all over but this generation of children will not take the tough subjects. Whether it's because they're not ready, whether it's because they're lazy, whether their 'social consciousness' took over and we're going to have a whole generation of 'socially conscious' people who are antitechnology—I don't know, but our supply line is stagnant and our demands are up."

What's worse, the supply line might be drying up in Ellis' own household. "I have a 12-year-old daughter and when we're sitting at the dinner table and I ask her what she's going to major in at college she'll answer 'social economics,' or some deal.

"I know she's only 12 years old and I should get off her back, but . . ." says Ellis in her Florida drawl. "And I ask her 'Why?' and she says 'Because I want to help people.' So I tell her, 'You'd be more help to people if you used your brain.' "

Benefiting From 'An Extraordinary Upbringing'

Ellis can attest from her own upbringing that the best way for girls to write their own job ticket is by using their brains; especially the left side of it. She comes from an extended family whose members believed that intelligence counts, whether you're paid to think or not.

"The people closest to me in my childhood were my grandmother, my Dad, and my Mom—in that order. All three consistently told us kids that we could do whatever we wanted to do if we worked hard enough. It wasn't a case of how much money you had, or who you knew, but what was between your ears and how you applied it."

Ellis avers that the women who wind up as successes in business do so because of an extraordinary upbringing, not merely by working in a female-friendly environment: "It's how you're raised and what you think you can do versus what everybody tells you you can do."

"From the time my grandmother was 16 years old she ran a hotel in a small town in Florida. My mother, on the other hand, never had a job until I graduated from high school. She was brought up to believe that women should learn everything possible but being from an old Southern family she felt they shouldn't have to work for a living—because that meant the husband wasn't worth 10 cents. So she had a great pride in everyone being well-educated but a very narrow view of what you did with it.

"Nevertheless, my mother's the one today who at 80 runs four miles a day and wants to go out in space with Walter Cronkite. So even though she didn't work she has a very broad-minded approach to life."

Learning Discipline and Teamwork from Childhood Activities

Ellis might have ended up on stage as a prima ballerina and not behind a desk as a high-tech executive had her father permitted her to go to New York to study ballet.

"I danced ballet for about eight years starting when I was six. I had a scholarship to study ballet in New York when I was eleven, but outside of my mother my family didn't want me to go. Southerners don't want their kids in New York."

While Ellis may have passed up a career in front of the klieg lights, the grueling daily regime to keep herself 'on her toes' was ideal preparation for the grueling college grind ahead as a double major and later as a single-parent executive.

"Ballet taught me an extreme amount of discipline and perseverance—because practicing ballet three to four hours a day hurts. There's no other word to put on it. And most ballet teachers are Atilla the Huns when it comes to pushing you to your limits, they're like swimming coaches whose basic message is, 'You know you can swim five more laps! Go out there and drown!' When I did ballet I never watched TV, I just went to school, studied, did ballet and went to sleep."

When Ellis was fourteen her father, a regional manager with Uniroyal, was transferred to Atlanta.

"So here I was in Atlanta with hours a day on my hands. So I started playing sports: basketball, softball, tennis, and track. I had a great coach in high school who instilled in me that I could do all this although I had never done it before."

If ballet taught her discipline, Ellis says that participating in team sports prepared her to be a team leader in the business world.

"I know women hate to hear this but I think high school sports gets you very ready for business, it really helps you understand how to pull people together as a team on the job. Ballet didn't prepare me for that at all."

Making Practical But Tough Educational Choices

Inspired by her high school math teacher, Ellis chose math as her major when she entered the University of Georgia in the fall of 1965. "But math got so theoretical—I had a course that taught you that one and one did *not* equal two—that I decided I was wasting my Dad's money at that point. I did not care why one and one did not equal two so that's when I started taking up statistics because it was real.

"So that gave me a double major. And doing math and statistics was hard. There were times during college when I thought: 'Why in the world am I doing this?' It's hard! But again, I was taught a great deal of perseverance so I made it."

In addition to taking two tough majors, she taught herself to program in Cobol, reading the manual straight through. "I knew I had to master that skill to get a job in the 1970s," she told an interviewer.

After a stint programming computers in Florida, Ellis moved to the Silicon Valley in 1976 and talked her way into a job at Fairchild Camera and Instrument Corp. She left there for Intel in 1980. "And everywhere I have worked for the most part it's been all men except me and at most one other woman."

Making It as an Innovator

When Ellis came to work in Intel's information services department she distinguished herself at the $3.2 billion semiconductor maker, not just as a problem solver, but an innovator as well. She piloted a system that permitted "computer-illiterate" individuals in various departments to access pertinent data via an information center; a primitive precursor to the personal computer. For example, the sales department might request a certain segment of its customer list from the computer in order to do a targeted mailing. In the past, each department would have had to ask the programmers to write a program to get the data, and then "wait in line," grumbling all the while, for the work to get done. Now they could access the data themselves.

Ellis had pitched the idea of information centers to Fairchild's management without much success. But her boss at Intel was intrigued. He was also skeptical that it could be made user-friendly.

"He told me, 'I don't think it will ever work. I don't think people can access their own data; they're going to have to have real programmers to help them.' "

Ellis made him a deal. "I said, 'I'll tell you what, you give me the money and resources and I'll make you a bet that in a year we'll have a live demo.' And I pulled it off."

Ellis attests that there's nothing more exhilarating than accomplishing something nobody thinks you can. "Let's face it, that's a really big high—taking something that's hard to do and that nobody else is doing and pulling it off."

Transforming Losers Into Winners: Turning Around a Failing Division

Ellis disdains the notion that the only way to advance in your career is by proving yourself in the revenue-generating areas of the company—the "line" jobs. She cites as one of her biggest accomplishments revitalizing Intel's customer service division as its manager in 1983, a unit whose primary function at most companies is not making money, but making excuses.

On a scale of "lemon" assignments, this one was a grapefruit: she was the third manager in three years. Her first challenge wasn't just learning a new area of the business but managing people who didn't exactly view themselves as vital to Intel's bottom line.

"These people were 'talked at' and were being jerked around

daily on their job duties: There was no strategic plan, no vision, no "win" defined—no nothin.' They just came to work every day, made excuses for Intel and went home dead.

"And I said, this is no way to run a business. Since I was used to managing very highly paid technical people I decided I was going to treat the customer service people like they were real people."

She also redefined customer service as a solution function and not a 'making excuses' function: "Getting to the root of the problem and finding the people in the company who can really fix the problems rather than just report them."

"When I left the job a year later we had a group that was energized, owned their own fate, and thought they made decisions that made a difference."

Adding To The Career Tool Kit— Diversifying For Success

In 1990, Ellis was named Vice-President of Human Resources after having served since 1988 as Vice-President of the Administration Group, overseeing Intel's internal computer needs, facilities, materials, human resources, and international finance and administration.

After more than two decades working and managing in data processing, Ellis doesn't worry that she's taken a career detour heading up human resources, because unlike most women she's already "done time" in the technical areas of the business where women typically fear to tread.

"I'm just the opposite of most women: I have all the required background to go toe-to-toe with anybody on technology. I've got the technical stuff behind me and I've got a lot of management time behind me, along with having handled customer services and administration. I know who I am, I know what I can do and I know what I've done."

Ellis takes an "equal opportunity" approach to problem-solving, it doesn't matter if you're working on the staff or line side as long as it's a challenge and you're up to the challenge.

"Heading up HR adds to my tool kit. In taking this job I

took an assignment that was one of the top five priorities in the company: to move an area ahead that was stalled in neutral. So if you take on the risky deals that matter to the business, and you leave them in a lot better shape than when you found them you will get ahead. That's what we all get paid to do."

Taking Responsibility For Your Career Advancement

As head of human resources, one of Ellis' responsibilities is dealing with the glass ceiling issues at Intel. When interviewed for this book in November 1991, she was hoping to meet with federal Labor Secretary Lynn Martin to discuss the issue. Not surprisingly, as a woman who has climbed the ladder by taking the "tough subjects" she's not too keen on the notion of women playing the corporate game "with a handicap."

Even at the dinner table, Ellis makes it clear to her daughter, Stephanie, that women have to take the responsibility to make themselves worthy of advancement, and the company's job is more akin to acting as a referee, blowing the whistle on any fouls.

"Who 'owns' your career advancement? I say from my vantage point as head of HR that the employee owns 51 percent of it and the company owns 'helping you accomplish the other 49 percent'. The employee owns 'doing what she likes to do' but she also owns 'being very good at what she does and getting the skills that are needed on the street.'

"If women really want to knock 'em dead in business they've got to understand the law of supply and demand. That means if a woman wants to major in social work in college and there's a 10-to-1 ratio of social work graduates to social work jobs, my advice to her is to look at the needs of the workplace and reconsider. Secondly, you've got to be the best at what you do. If you aim to be the best you can be, and if your skills matter to the companies that are hiring you're going to do pretty well. The woman 'owns' those two aspects of her career and the company can't accomplish them for her.

"Many women's groups would argue that you've got to put

an 'advantage system' in place to cancel out the disadvantage against women. I disagree. I believe that what the company 'owns' is putting a level playing field in place for advancement. A woman puts her skills on the table, she puts her track record on the table, she runs the race. The best person wins. Period."

Don't get her wrong, Ellis doesn't argue against the existence of the glass ceiling. But she says there's a big difference between creating an artificial "hothouse"environment to stimulate the career growth of women and blowing the whistle when talented, worthy women are not being considered for management jobs.

"The way I see the glass ceiling issue is that if at a certain company there are no women on the executive staff or who are general managers, regional managers, or plant managers something's wrong. And what you've got to do is find out what's wrong. Unfortunately, the higher you get in management the more complex the decisions become whether or not to promote people. At these levels, determining who wins the race is less clear cut."

Two-Career Sacrifices

Ellis also believes that it's wrong for companies to put an "advantage" system in place when it comes to international assignments, which would translate into waiving such a requirement for executive women because relatively few of them are married to stay-at-home husbands or ones with "portable" careers. Here her byword is: equal opportunity sacrifice.

"If a husband or a wife really wants to get to the top, guess what! Not one of you but both of you are going to give up something on the way. I think a couple has to sit down and decide what sacrifice in your lifestyle each career opportunity is going to cause you to make, how it's going to alter your life. The end result may be a trailing husband, it may be a trailing wife, it may be a commuter marriage, it may be an I-don't-want-the-job. But for each opportunity there's a cost; there's no free lunch in life."

But she maintains that nobody, man or woman, should expect to get the top job if he or she has always got an eye on the clock as well as the prize. As a single parent of a son and a daughter in elementary school, she compares the grueling schedule of the members of Intel's executive staff with that of her own.

"When I consider the relatively few days during a given month that the members of the executive staff are even home to kiss their children goodnight I can't exactly complain because sometimes I don't get home for dinner. Believe me, if you interviewed my kids they'd say I give too much to Intel. But compared to some other people, I don't give as much. When you take a job you have to decide what's going to give."

Corporate Day Care: Is It Realistic?

Not surprisingly, if Ellis isn't too keen on an "advantage" system for career women, she isn't going to cotton to the notion of Intel anteing up for a corporate day care center, just because it's somebody's notion that it might make working mothers feel less guilty about working.

"As much as I'd love a place downstairs where my six-year-old son Jason could ride in with me three days a week and I could have lunch with him, I think it's impractical. I don't believe it solves the problem for working parents and we don't have it here—although we do have a child care referral program.

"Let's put Intel on the line; we don't do programs out of fear. We operate on good, solid data. We're a data company, we're a computing company, and the data tells us that in an area like Silicon Valley where people live in a 50-mile radius of work they do not want to pull their kids out of neighborhood schools and activities to bring them to work.

"Secondly, we have 23,000 employees and my guess is that we have 35,000 kids flung all over the world. Where in the world would we put a day care center to take care of 35,000 children?"

Closing the Wage Gap—Offering Alternative Work Styles

One way that human resources departments can create a level playing field for women is by creating a level "paying field."

Studies show that even at management levels a wage gap of up to 40 percent exists between men and women doing the same work.

"Equal pay for equal work to me is common sense, so let's do it. Clearly for no other reason than we should be paying for 'mips' of brain power versus anything else, we need to figure out what a job is, benchmark a job no matter who has it and pay the person what the job is worth. Period.

"Secondly, and just as importantly, I think we have to offer a menu of job types to accommodate different workstyles. And what does that mean? Job-sharing, part-time, work-from-home, extended leave—I guess that covers it. And let's not make people feel like they're a three-headed attraction at the circus if they want to do that."

Job-sharing isn't a touchy-feely, good-for-employees issue, Ellis declares, it's simply good for business.

"What are corporations trying to do today? Get more done! So to me, there's a bottom line result here. There are statistics on the table today that show that people who share a job create more output than one person doing the job. There's also data that says if you've got a person working part-time, half-time, or two-thirds time they do a full-time job anyway. Because when they're here, they're hurrying to get the job done because they know they've got to leave soon versus just putting in the time."

Ellis conjectures that a major reason why more employees don't participate in alternative workstyle arrangements is that they don't pay enough.

"If wages are low anyway, who can take 'half of low'? What does it take to solve the problem? Companies need to take a dramatic review of the job structures, job descriptions, and salary scales. The 1940s wage system is not going to work. So there should be a level salary for jobs; level meaning the right salary for the right reasons.

"And as I told Felice Schwartz, this is not a woman-only issue and I would appreciate it if she would not treat it that way. The solution has to be looked at as a broad-based 'how-do-you-do-work' approach, versus the approach of 'Oh, we've got to throw in this program so that females of the world will quit bitchin.' "

PART THREE

Refusing to Play the Game:

Deciding When to Fight and When to Switch

Introduction—When To Fight vs. When To Switch

For the eleven women whose career paths we've just followed, there are basic rules that seem to work across the board. Melissa Cadet's self-empowering "mantra" is similar to Carlene Ellis' belief that the employee "owns" 51% of the progress of her success. Whether by verbalizing or serving as a role model, these women have told us it is imperative to be proactive while charting the course to top management.

Other patterns leap out of these pages: There is the readiness to make lemonade out of a "lemon" assignment, such as Linda Wroblewski's eagerness to jump at the chance to oversee a new department at Laventhol & Horwath that male colleagues had turned down; there is the ability to turn aside the peccadilloes of resentful coworkers or subordinates in order to gain something greater—these women don't fight every fight, they pick and choose. They are willing to use smokescreens if it means they'll land a client, even though it means hiding their authority or using, as Karen Reimer does, "an alter ego." They play the game, that old cliche, but they are still gaining success from it. Overall, they tell us that it's important to stay focused on what's important.

And their career stories point out the healthy future for a diversified workplace. The fact that the old boys club will not be able to thrive is never clearer than when we see how different cultures and genders add spice to our industry's future. These newcomers' ability to see things in a different way threads throughout these stories—from Shirley Prutch, the pioneer, who handled the problem of communicating with employees about to undergo lay-offs sympathetically, or Jacquie Arthur who knew when to make employees feel a part of the process.

But what if you are proactive, don't take no for an answer, deal assertively with resentful subordinates and coworkers, are a master at turning aside sexual innuendoes or overtures—all the right moves—and yet still you feel like you are banging your head against that old glass ceiling?

In short, what happens if you still aren't getting where you want to go? Let's face it, life isn't always fair, and nowhere is that more apparent than in the business world.

One option is to sue your company, as Ann Hopkins sued Price Waterhouse in 1984—and won in 1990. She tells her story in Chapter 16. Chapter 17 provides further guidance on filing a lawsuit based on sex discrimination: what to expect in terms of reward, what to consider before you sue, how to file a complaint and a lawsuit, and what laws protect women from sex discrimination.

But before considering a lawsuit, many women seek an alternative career path. Chapter 15 profiles three women who are on the lower rungs of the career ladder and have experienced the kind of job frustrations that can send women heading for the exits. These women are dealing with sex discrimination by taking a different path to career satisfaction: They've chosen job satisfaction over the climb for the top job.

chapter **15**

LESSONS FROM THE TRENCHES: CHOOSING ALTERNATIVE CAREER PATHS

No book about successful career women would be complete without querying those who are still on the lower rungs of the ladder, many of whom decide to get off.

For one thing, the pool of top-ranking female executives is so small that we can't rely on their personal insights alone to determine why more women aren't getting to the top; only 19 women rank among the highest paid officers among the nation's 800 largest companies.

For another, many of the women who do succeed don't actually "shatter" the glass ceiling barring women from management jobs, but are brought in over it by courageous male executives who recognized their talents and didn't care whether or not the other men in the inner circle were "ready" for women to join it. A few of the women profiled in the previous section acknowledge that they fit in this category.

For the most part, women who continually face career frustrations "solve" the problem by bailing out because the nicest thing about no longer banging your head against the ceiling is that it feels so good when you stop.

They bail out either by shifting their career expectations from a *powerful* job to a *meaningful* job or by downsizing their choice of employers to a smaller company, where *what* an employee knows usually is more valuable than *who* they know in high places. Or these women sever the cord to corporate America entirely and start their own companies.

A study called Don't Blame the Baby published in May 1990 by Wick & Co., a Wilmington, Delaware consulting firm, revealed that as a result of career frustrations only 35% of women say they'll stay in their current job, compared to 77% of men.

According to Victoria Tashjian, the Wick Vice-President who conducted the study, what frustrates women as much as the "actionable" acts of discrimination is being treated as if they were invisible—or, at best, inconsequential. "You're not being taken seriously, you're not a member of the team, your comments are discounted, your opinion is not asked for. It's all very subtle, it's not intentional, it's part of everyone's pro-gramming—but it works a vicious circle in that the woman discounts herself, perhaps questions her own ideas.

"If after a period of time a woman feels more and more like she's not getting a return on her investment, that's when she decides that she's going to make a change," says Tashjian. "So like it or not, Mr. Corporate CEO, if you want to keep women in your organization you've got to realize that unless they're getting the payback, they're more likely than men to leave."

This chapter is devoted to airing the frustrations of those women who are nowhere near cracking the glass ceiling, but whose insights are every bit as valuable as the women who are. Along with the affronts that are classically defined as sex dis-crimination, such as being passed over unfairly for a promo-tion, there are three workplace frustrations that rank high on the list of career aggravations for women: I have dubbed them The Pat on the Head, The Pat on the Tummy, and Surrogate Wives.

Dealing With 'The Pat on the Head'

One of the reasons why Jeanne Rice left a job in corporate America to become a freelance writer is because she got sick of being treated like somebody's daughter.[52]

"I once attended a meeting with five senior executives. I participated, offered thoughts, contributed ideas, and asked questions. I felt good. I felt productive. But within moments, my confidence was shattered.

"As I turned to walk out the door, I overheard one executive exclaim to the others: 'Isn't she just so cute? I'd love to fix her up with my son!' "

Rice cites another example of a colleague of hers who is responsible for advising management on all levels of corporate communications. The woman attended a meeting of a senior officer in which he critiqued a project, not knowing it was hers. When she thanked him for the feedback, he was flustered: "I would never have criticized it if I had known you had written it! I would have never been so hard on a young lady!"

There are very few more frustrating experiences for a woman than receiving the psychological equivalent of a pat on the head—praise for a contribution but no recognition, as described by Judy Frank later in this chapter.

When Judy Frank asked the president of her company whether she'd be tapped for a promotion to vice-president, his reaction was to give her a title, not the job. "They gave me a 'token' title of Assistant Vice-President and patted me on the head, virtually saying, 'Be a good girl, you're an Assistant Vice-President at a relatively young age: 27, 28, or whatever. And I had to admit it worked for about three months. I thought, 'Yeah, well this is really nice. I think I can probably work this situation through.' "

Dealing With 'The Pat on the Tummy'

While much has been written about the effects of pregnancy on female hormones, not enough has been said about the psychological reactions produced in some men who work with pregnant women: wanting to mother the working mother.

Susan Cross, a lawyer at First Interstate Bancorp in Los Angeles said that when she got pregnant a male client suddenly started apologizing for swearing in her presence. A male co-worker asked her if she'd be able to walk to a nearby meeting—even though she already walked two miles a day for exercise.[53]

Perhaps Robin Piccone, President of Piccone Apparel Corp. in Los Angeles, received the ultimate patronizing act: the tummy pat (and note—she's President!). Piccone was six months pregnant when she showed her company's body glove swimwear line to store buyers. One male buyer reached out to rub her stomach goodbye.[54]

These patronizing acts are annoying, but not necessarily career stopping. Unfortunately, they can get worse. Judy Frank reports that once she became a mother, her new status sent a signal to a former boss that she wasn't able to carry out her job duties, despite her protestations.

Frank cites an instance when he sent her home to be with her child one evening when they were working against a deadline to complete a crucial company project.

"We had rearranged all of our employee benefits countrywide and had developed a video as part of a communications program. And one night at about 7 o'clock, we're about finished and he said to me, 'Why don't you go home?'

"And I said, 'I can stay, I've got my son taken care of,' and he said, 'No, no you go home.'

"And the next morning I said, 'Did you get finished?' And he said, 'Yeah, we got finished in another half an hour.' "

Frank found out later he'd been lying—the staff had finished more than three hours later—at 10 P.M.

"I know he probably thought, 'Oh, gee, she ought to be home with her child' and all of that but that's not what *I* thought. And it really bothered me. My reaction was 'Don't protect me.' "

It's bad enough when your boss doesn't take you seriously as a pregnant executive; it's quite another matter when your subordinates don't. Research confirms that many men have a tough time reconciling the image of a pregnant woman as boss. In a study by Philadelphia psychologist Sara Corse, business school students were asked to evaluate a pregnant boss compared to one who wasn't. Corse found that the students had expected the pregnant manager to be passive, nice and giving and were surprised by her authoritative behavior.[55]

Working With 'Wife Surrogates'

Often the working women who rubber-stamp the ideas of management, rather than offering ideas of their own, are the ones who get promoted. These women are in effect surrogate wives, not equal members of the team.

Both Beth Smiley and Judy Frank interviewed in this chapter and Honeywell's Karen Reimer profiled in Chapter 4 lament that often competent women are passed over in favor of "token" incompetent women.

Smiley described how such an individual got leapfrogged from a lowly writing job to Vice-President of Communications at her Fortune 500 manufacturing company—distinguishing her as the only female VP in a several thousand-employee corporation.

"She does not deserve to be there; she does not sit as an equal partner at the table. She had no previous supervisory experience. (Her boss) decided to 'bring her along,' she never really had to do a whole heck of a lot."

The upshot: rather than setting a standard for other women in the company, Smiley says, the shear blatancy of her incompetence causes the image of women to suffer.

"Whenever she says anything in a meeting the (other executives) roll their eyes. The other day she made a recommendation regarding company policy and when somebody asked for her rationale, she said, 'Because it's just good for our people.' You don't justify business decisions that way."

Judy Frank describes a surrogate wife at one of her previous employers who apparently was hired for her looks rather than her talents. "She'd cruise into the office a half an hour, forty-five minutes late and she'd sit there all day at work reading her Talbot's catalogue—she had them delivered to her desk. And it would drive me nuts to walk by her desk."

Frank says men who promote surrogate wives "sit there and pat themselves on the back and say, 'I have done a good thing.' But they haven't. I would never, never want to be promoted over a man if he deserved the job."

A Different Vantage Point: Alternative Career Paths

The following are the career sagas of three women, all of whom are in their mid-30s: Beth Smiley, Human Resources Manager of a Fortune 500 diversified manufacturer; Judy Frank, Director of Human Resources at a museum; and Barbara Williams, Internal Communications Director at an insurance company. Unlike the female executives profiled in Part II, I've given these women pseudonyms and left out the identities of their employers.

I selected these three women because they have a different view of success: they've chosen personal satisfaction with their job over vying for a crack at top management. Beth Smiley is working to destroy the glass ceiling by changing her company's personnel policies; Judy Frank found happiness at a smaller company, and Barbara Williams gained satisfaction by finding a low-profile job that stimulates her intellectually and allows her to travel, resolving that she'd rather be at peace with herself than play politics.

Beth Smiley: Destroying the Glass Ceiling

After less than two years at her current employer, an east coast Fortune 500 manufacturer, Beth Smiley at age 33 has risen to the position of manager of a unit in human resources. For Smiley the title represents a just reward for being a "squeaky wheel"; she griped about the way women were being treated and now she's part of a team that makes sure women don't get shunted aside.

"I was brought here as a clean sweeper; they sent me into the organization to help change it. That's how I am shattering the glass ceiling."

Smiley had first-hand experience at dealing with an unenlightened boss when she first joined the company in 1988 as Strategic Planning Manager of a $12 million unit after six years as a Management Consultant at a CPA firm and three years in the Army.

Smiley describes herself as "a very, very self-confident person—a nice person, but self-confident. I think that scares some people."

One of the first people she scared was her boss. In a word,

he was "an S.O.B. This guy was insecure and intimidated by me—intimidated by the fact that I had been a big-shot consultant for six years and that I was a female and that I drove a nice car. And he criticized me for everything, from the kind of car that I drove to the fact that I would wear grey or black suits to work when he would wear sweaters."

It didn't take long before her boss' daily harangues undermined Smiley's productivity, not to mention her state of mind. "I couldn't think straight. All I could think about was what is this guy going to do to me next?"

After three months, she couldn't take any more abuse and resolved to go over the man's head. She marched into the president's office—"who I just happened to know because I believe in saying 'hi' to everybody"—prepared to hand in her resignation.

"I said to him, 'I'm going to leave the company, I'll do it very quietly, but I want to tell you why.'

"So I told him what this guy was doing to me. And I was almost in tears—it was the first time in my career that I've been that close to tears."

Being a newcomer to corporate politics, in which the "politically correct" reaction to a subordinate who is complaining about his or her boss is to side with the boss, Smiley was not exactly prepared for the president's suggestion.

"He said, 'Have you gone to lunch with this guy?'

Smiley was flabbergasted. "I told him, 'No. And I'm not going to lunch with this guy.'"

"He said, 'How do you think you can work this out?'

"And I said, 'I'm not! I'm not going to work it out.'

"He was acting like *I* had done something wrong! And I wasn't convinced that I had done anything wrong.

"He asked if I could go back and give it one more try. I said, 'Okay, I'll try it for one more week and then I'll talk to you.' And he agreed to that."

Somehow, word of her session with the president had trickled down to her boss. He was not pleased.

"He called me into his office, called me on the carpet, telling me how incompetent I was. He was going on and on and on."

Smiley had been keeping a journal at her desk in which she would record her boss' remarks, so she decided that now would be as good a time as any to update it.

"So I got out a pad and paper and said, 'Wait a minute, Marty, I want to get all this down. What are these things that you're accusing me of here?'

"So he said, 'You don't have to write this down.' And I answered, 'Oh, yes I do. I've never been accused of these things before . . .'

"And he said, 'Well you ought to get out of here before I fire you.' I told him I didn't think he would fire me but if that made him feel more powerful he could do that. I had only been there three months, I had nothing to lose."

After the face-off, Smiley took a couple of personal days off because she didn't want to be around her boss. When she returned, she went back to the president of the company and said, "Sorry, this isn't going to work."

The upshot: Smiley was reassigned to the division's headquarters to become a business planner for that division. Unfortunately, she was flipped from the frying pan into the fire: one of her first duties as a business planner was to eliminate the very unit she worked for. So she faced joblessness after only a few months on the job.

Smiley was walking down the hall one day mulling over her career options, when a personnel executive she knew only vaguely exchanged pleasantries with her.

"When he asked me how I was doing, I was bold enough to say, 'Not too good. I don't have a job right now. I do excellent work, I'm a great manager, and I can't believe this is happening to me.'

"And he said, 'Can you be down in my office in 15 minutes?' He's an action-oriented person."

The man turned out to be her mentor in disguise. He helped Smiley get a job as "Manager of Training and Development" in the personnel area. From all appearances, Smiley's job is one of the few human resources jobs in the country that actually carries some clout in the corridors of power, a job that she got because "I criticized a consultant's report that talked about all the wonderful things that the company was doing for the diverse workforce. My reaction: 'This is baloney, because it only talks about numbers and programs and not what the company is doing to recognize women.' "

One of her responsibilities is to evaluate top management's choice of employees who have fast-track potential. Smiley says that when the company's top brass first prepared a list of candidates, all the names on it "were all the buddies of these guys. So we said, 'Okay, scratch that list. Now we want you to look at who really is capable of these positions.' And they came back with a totally different list with a couple of women and a couple of minorities on it. So when they're forced to look at management qualities they may choose women and minorities, however the first choice is always someone of their own demographic background."

Despite having moved quickly up the ladder in such a short time, Smiley isn't interested in the CEO's job or anything close to it. "I don't like the lifestyle of a CEO. You're not running a company, you're trying to raise money or you're trying to convince the stockholders that you are worth their investment. Big deal.

"Ultimately I'd like to have my own company, go off on my own and do consulting. I'm not interested in how much turf I have or how much money I manage. It doesn't matter to me."

Judy Frank: Finding the Right Company

The veteran of six jobs since graduating from college in the late 1970s, Judy Frank believes she's finally reached her career goals and peace of mind at the same time. Frank doesn't mind that she's not on a fast track; she's found personal satisfaction as Director of Human Resources for a museum in the Northeast.

"As Director of Human Resources, I'm in a fairly traditional female role," Frank said. "But my goal was always to head up human resources, I didn't care whether I was CEO of a company. My feeling was that if you were at the right company, certainly the head of human resources was going to be a very valuable and sought after job—if you're at the right company."

Simply finding the right company entailed having to work for a lot of the wrong kinds of bosses first. Frank got a sense of the obstacles she would be facing throughout her career at her second job when her boss, the Vice-President of Human Resources at the bank, retired after many years of service and the job was awarded not to Frank but a male colleague she believes was far less deserving.

Frank was instead given the job of "Assistant Vice-President" which is a common ploy used by management when they don't want a woman in the top job but they don't want to risk affronting her (and, perhaps, inviting a lawsuit) with a blatant turn-down. This is a "maybe later" tactic, an attempt to assuage the woman's ego that after some unidentified interval of time she can qualify for management. But, like Sisyphus, the mythical Greek king condemned to an afterlife in Hades pushing a rock up a steep grade, only to have it fall back again, "later" never becomes "now."

Losing the promotion was a body blow from which it took her years to recover. "I felt—I can't even describe it, I was so overwhelmed. I felt betrayed. I just couldn't believe it. That's when I first experienced the shock to my system that even though you work hard, you're productive, and you're contributing quality stuff, you don't necessarily succeed. It really hit home."

Frank says there's no question her qualifications far surpassed those of the man who was tapped for the job: "My credentials and the quality of work I had produced for the company was significantly better."

She just didn't have all the right moves. Frank realizes now that her male counterpart was tapped for the promotion because he knew how to play the game.

"He was a single guy; he played poker with management on Wednesday night and went drinking with the guys on Thursday night"—not the kinds of activities that women get invited to—certainly not respectable married women like Frank who are supposed to be home with their husbands and/or kids after work. "I was probably naive politically. When I looked at that situation, I didn't play by the rules."

Not that Frank wasn't ready and willing to "hang out" with the guys. She insists she loves sports and can bandy about RBI's and league standings with the best of them. But she also knows that if she dared make overtures to do so, she'd be misinterpreted. "I love sports—I love college basketball and I can talk sports."

But she says it's impossible to ask the guys to lunch where these casual conversations are made "because people think you're going to have an affair with them."

Frank says her second tactical error was working long hours at her job instead of simply working more visible hours. Her male colleague would "cruise into work at 8:30 A.M. and stayed until 6 or 6:30 so he made himself visible. I'm married, an early morning person; I'll come in at 7:30 and work till 5:30."

After three months at her token Assistant Vice-President job, working under a man who knew less about managing than she did, "I decided I couldn't learn anything from this guy. I just felt that for my own sanity I needed to try to move on."

Her next career move was a lateral one to the employee benefits area of a Fortune 500 chemical company, "And I had a super male boss. But *his* boss was the problem."

Frank's next on-the-job lesson in male psychology was learning that even when you do find a male boss who feels comfortable with a woman, don't be surprised if the friendship makes another man jealous.

Her boss' superior "didn't like it because he felt that my boss and I had too good a relationship, we worked really well together. And it really bothered him because he and my boss had sort of been buddies before I came."

The big boss' solution? He found his own female "pet."

"Another woman was hired shortly after I was whom the big boss took under his wing. His attitude was that if my boss was going to have a 'pet' then he was going to have a pet! And it got really silly; it got a little tense around the office."

Things got more than tense when Frank became pregnant with her first child. "The big boss literally stopped talking to me when I got pregnant. Then he didn't want to give me my old job back after my maternity leave because I wanted to take longer than six weeks off." The handwriting was now on the wall in large block letters: Time to job hunt again.

Looking back, she wonders why as a human resources expert she didn't follow the advice she gives others to try to rectify her job situation internally.

"Sometimes I think, 'What a jerk I was.' I should have known better: I should have exhausted my resources within the company to improve my job situation before deciding to leave, which is what I always advise people."

On the other hand, her employer was "a Fortune 500 chemical company and we're not talking about a lot of opportunities for advancement for women because there simply weren't a lot of women working there."

It took her three more employers before Frank could find job satisfaction. Finally, in her current post as Director of Human Resources for a 500-employee museum, she says "I finally have everything I want. There's a lot of really bright, intellectual people. And my boss is absolutely incredible."

For one thing, she didn't have to concern herself that her current boss would ice her out or start patronizing her when she decided to get pregnant again.

"After the experience with my first child I waited a long time to have another child. This time, when I went to my boss and told him I was pregnant, he smiled and said, 'I couldn't be happier for you. I hope you don't leave us.' And I said, 'Oh, no, I'll come back.' "

Frank says she's finally found career peace of mind. She says that her definition of career success isn't measured by her personal power or the revenues of her employer but "I realize that it has to be a personal success."

Barbara Williams: Stopped Playing the Game

Barbara Williams, 36, works in corporate communications at a large Northeast-based multinational insurance company. She is primarily responsible for writing "this company's version of *People* magazine. I absolutely love what I do."

Even though she doesn't always love the people that she does it for.

Armed with a degree in broadcast journalism, Williams job-hopped a half a dozen times before she found her current job, for the most part because her then-husband relocated frequently. She worked in radio for seven years, at a school for emotionally disturbed adolescents, a state children's department, a United Way child care agency, and the Girl Scouts of America before coming to work for her current employer three years ago.

Williams says that it was only recently that she has come to grips with the limits to her career potential, like many women of her generation who initially believed that the civil rights movement and the women's movement had created sufficient momentum to reverse workplace inequities.

"As a child of the sixties, I was convinced all the trails had been blazed and that I was going to be judged purely on my abilities and would not encounter any problems. Until I came to this company, where I am functioning in a purely male dominated environment and now I'm in touch with reality. What frustrates me the most is that the men here just haven't a clue that I would have any aspirations, ambitions, talents, or capabilities. I have to remind them."

Williams has found that getting a "good grade" on your annual job evaluation may buy you a little job security but it won't get you a better job. This falls under the "pat on the head" syndrome described earlier in this chapter.

"We had a system to identify 'fast-trackers'—people who would be put on a track to become Assistant Vice-President, say, within five years. And a group of 10 management people would decide once a year which employees should be put into this group, whose members were eligible to receive as much as double the approved salary raise.

"Following my appraisal last year after two years at the company, I said to my boss, 'What do I need to do to be considered for this group?'

"And he stared at me with a kind of blank look on his face and he said, 'Well, I never thought of you for that.'

"I said, 'I know you don't think of me in that regard, that's why I'm asking.' "

The light went on in her boss' brain.

"He said, 'Now that I think about it, you exhibit all the same tendencies that we look for. I'm going to recommend you.' "

Unfortunately, Williams' boss didn't realize—or forgot—that the very tendencies that are highly esteemed in a man spell trouble when they're exhibited by a woman. She was turned down.

The "group of 10" apparently argued that Williams was "abrasive and emotional."

Williams' voice rises in anger as she derides the irony in the assessment. "Now, this is a company that rewards entrepreneurial behavior. This is a company that has emotional European men working for it. This is a company where raised voices in the hallway are *de rigeur*. But when *I'm* emotional or entrepreneurial, it's a negative."

In Williams' estimation, it's not surprising that management doesn't know what to make of her aspirations when they seem to have a hard time judging what it's going to take to attract women to a company in the first place.

One of her superiors asked Williams to make a presentation at a worldwide conference on the subject of attracting and retaining women as insurance agents and agency managers. She had heard the request before.

"Two years ago they said they wanted a story on that very issue in the magazine that I edit and I responded, 'Excuse me. I can't write that article. As long as you view recruiting women as a separatist kind of thing you're never going to achieve what you want to achieve.'

Her advice instead was to appeal to women by touting the very same attractions about selling life insurance that appeal to men: "autonomy, unlimited earnings potential, write-your-own-schedule. And when I said that they looked at me like I was from Pluto. Or speaking a foreign language. Because in their minds, they should be talking to women about issues like day care. Baloney!"

Williams says she's had lots of wonderful discussions with women on this question in the Middle East and with women of Indian and Asian descent who work in the U.K. division—women one might assume would be more "traditional" in their thinking. "They laugh at me," Williams says, when she tells them management's view of what women really want.

Williams realizes that she's not going to change male attitudes overnight; a realization that came after years of job-hopping and resigning herself to the fact that the grass always winds up being just as weed-infested on the other side of the fence. Her inner debate has centered instead around whether she's going to play the game by the boys' rules or warm the bench—but keep her integrity and peace of mind.

"For a long time I really believed that being good, being the best that I could be would pay off in the long run. But in the corporate environment I have discovered that being good has very little to do with it. Being astute politically and able to play the game are perceived as far more important skills than being able to do the job.

"I'm convinced at this stage that no matter where you go there's going to be a certain level of frustration. There is no perfect place, there is no nirvana. It's all a set of trade-offs."

So while Williams puts up with a lack of power and respect,

she also enjoys a degree of freedom that somebody with a great deal of power might envy.

"I get to travel internationally, I have a great deal of autonomy, I'm exposed to the highest levels of the company—if I were in a larger company I'd be buried in some morass of an external affairs department.

"No, the public relations track does not lead to the CEO's office. And I don't aspire to be CEO. That's a conscious decision that I made. I'm at peace with myself."

Ann Hopkins
of Price Waterhouse:

SUING HER COMPANY FOR SEX DISCRIMINATION

During the 1960s and 1970s when feminists were debating whether women should hang out with a multitude of sexual partners, Ann Hopkins was working for IBM figuring out how to make satellites hang out in the sky properly.

"I am not a movement person or a joiner," declares the management consultant.[56] "I've been cast as a role model but I've never thought of myself as one."[57]

But in the 1980s Hopkins was nonetheless responsible for bringing the most significant sex discrimination lawsuit of the decade.

When in May 1990 a federal judge ordered accounting firm Price Waterhouse to make her a partner and give her $370,000 in back pay, women's groups hailed the victory as a watershed among second-generation employment discrimination cases addressing the right of women to hold management positions. (The first generation, beginning in the 1960s, broke more blatant barriers to entering the workplace).

Lynn Hecht Schafran, a lawyer for NOW's Legal Defense Fund, called the judge's ruling "fabulous. It means women will be evaluated and valued by employers on the basis of the work product, not in terms of sex stereotypes."[58]

If you ask Hopkins why she sued Price Waterhouse, she'll invariably say, "I got an unsatisfactory explanation for an irrational business decision."

The irrational decision she's referring to occurred in 1982

when Hopkins and 87 male colleagues came up for consideration as partners. Although in the previous few years Hopkins had played a big part in securing some $40 million in contracts for the firm—an amount which she says was more than that of any other candidate for partner in 1982—she was not among the 47 people promoted.

In early 1983, Hopkins was told that the partnership decision had been delayed and a few months later she was informed that she would not be nominated. In 1984 she resigned and sued, claiming that the promotion process had violated Title VII of the 1964 Civil Rights Act, which prohibits job discrimination.

In his ruling, U.S. District Judge Gerhard A. Gesell ordered Price Waterhouse to admit her to the partnership as of July 1, 1990. Price Waterhouse subsequently appealed. Eventually, Hopkins returned to the company with her partnership.

Why She Sued: "You're Supposed to 'Behave Like a Woman' "

During her lawsuit, Hopkins learned about the psychological underpinnings of how irrational management decisions are made.

While she was nominated for partnership at age 38 because her "strong character, independence, and integrity are well recognized by her clients as well as her peers," the very qualities that enabled her to bring more money into the firm than anybody else vying for the job, were considered liabilities by some partners.

The court found particularly damning a remark made by Hopkins' mentor and chief supporter—in an ironic attempt to help her win over less enlightened partners: "He told me to walk more femininely, talk more femininely, wear makeup, have my hair styled, and wear jewelry," Hopkins said at the trial.

"What the courts have found is that when it comes to the partnership, which is more like a club, that I was evaluated not as a manager but as a woman and I didn't fit the stereotypical role of a woman," Hopkins says.

"The situation is a double bind. Suppose that a woman's approach to a business problem is 'We're going to take that goddam hill over there and if there are a few bodies along the way, tough'—which is one characteristic of the managerial norm—that's sort of the mindset you have to have to get the job done.

"But that approach is in conflict with this notion that you're supposed to 'behave like a woman,' which means that you're supposed to dress femininely, talk femininely, and be soft, warm, and lovable. So instead of being evaluated on the basis of results and on what you have accomplished, you're evaluated on a set of personality characteristics and whether or not they fit.

"It's not whether you're effective in getting the results, it's a question of whether you fit some view of what a wife or mistress or daughter or somebody ought to look like."

A Role Model Even in Her Early Years

Hopkins didn't have any particular career goals after graduating from Hollins College in Roanoke, Virginia, so she did what a lot of her friends did and continued her education, pursuing a Master's degree in mathematics from Indiana University.

"It was 1966–67, a time when graduate schools weren't real thrilled about taking women from women's colleges, where their experience is bad; in other words, women don't typically finish the program. I viewed it as my responsibility to finish because the next 'guy' might not get in if I don't get out."

So while Hopkins doesn't think of herself as a "movement" person, nonetheless she decided to do whatever she could to give her fellow female grad students the intestinal fortitude to complete the program.

"Since we were all in different disciplines, we didn't help each other academically, we'd have a few beers together or a cup of tea and kept each other in a sufficient psychological state so that we could get through this."

Climbing the Ladder at IBM and Touche Ross

Following graduation, after teaching briefly at Hollins, Hopkins traded in the academic world for the business world, joining IBM's Washington, D.C. federal systems division as system analyst.

For the next three or four years she managed a seven-person team at IBM that "worked with the effects of solar radiation, magnetic pressure, and aerodynamic pressure" on weather and scientific satellites.

"It was just about as good a job as you could possibly get if you happened to be interested in equations and things theoretical. However, I discovered that things theoretical were rather a lonely business. What's more, I want to work in the main line of a company's business. And software systems were not IBM's main line."

But neither was she happy working for various smaller software companies and ultimately followed a headhunter's advice to take her project management skills to Touche Ross. She joined the firm in 1974.

"They had an absolutely superb project management methodology and I had a marvelous time managing fascinating projects. One of them was putting in the medical claims processing system for the then 850,000-odd beneficiaries of the United Mine Workers health and retirement funds. I had a fascinating time—I've probably been in half of the coal mines in the country."

Coping With Difficult Attitudes Toward Working Mothers and a Two-Career Household

While working for Touche Ross, Hopkins also met her now exhusband and had a child. While she says she doesn't remember confronting noticeably backward views about women in any of her work situations before the partnership debacle in 1983, she does recall how some of her co-workers and clients had a tough time coping with the notion of a working mom in the mid-1970s.

"I had indicated that I was going to be out for a couple of weeks and I was going to be back after my daughter was born. But despite the fact that I ultimately turned out to be away from the office for three weeks people were preparing for my departure if I was going to die or be hit by a truck. Because nobody believed me."

The next "rather strange, very anachronistic, and not very modern policy" Hopkins confronted is they both couldn't be partners at the same time while they were both employed by Touche Ross.

And since both members of the couple were ambitious, one of them had to look for a new job. Because as a by-the-numbers "hard consultant," Hopkins was seen as more marketable than her husband, she decided she would be the one to quit. Her husband, who also had more seniority than she, went on to become a partner.

Achieving Success at Price Waterhouse

Hopkins left to work for another consulting firm, American Management Systems. But that wasn't the right fit, either.

"I came to the realization that underneath my T-shirt tattooed across my chest were the words 'Big Eight Management Consultant.' So she joined Price Waterhouse in 1978. After managing a project for the Bureau of Indian Affairs which involved a lot of jetting around the country visiting Indian reservations, she decided that she'd rather work closer to headquarters.

"In my business you get a lot of requests for proposals, RFPs, from the federal government. And as I was flying back and forth, I got one of these what-do-you-think's on a proposal from the State Department. I usually avoided RFPs like the plague because when you only have a 14 or 15-person outfit it's a little tough to be credible selling into the government market unless you pick things real carefully."

But this project sounded like it was do-able with a small staff. And it kept on being do-able while it grew like Topsy and required a larger staff.

"It was the tip of a very, very large iceberg. I spent the rest of my career at Price Waterhouse working with the State Department as a client on a job that went from $1 million or so to $40 or $50 million. And as this was going on, the office grew from some 14 or 15 people to hundreds of people, all in a span of three or four years.

"So I went from miners to Indians to diplomats. I got an absolutely remarkable set of results. When I sold the State Department project it was the largest piece of consulting work Price Waterhouse had ever had—and that's the nationwide firm. And I managed to do that in a humongous number of billable hours, which translates into bottom-line profits for the firm because the cost of sales weren't great compared to the billings. It's a great way to do business and it's normally the mark of a very accomplished consultant to be able to do it.

"So I was nominated for the partnership and the rest is history. I got the results. I just didn't get into the club."

"You Can't Go Home Again"—Why Hopkins Did

The first question on most people's minds following the outcome of the case is why go back to a company where the top brass seemingly values ineffectual feminine women over aggressive women who can make the company money?

For one thing, Hopkins points out, the number of female partners at the firm has grown since 1983, the year the lawsuit was filed—whether as a direct result of her lawsuit, or merely a function of changing times. By illustration, Hopkins talks about a party that was recently held for a woman in the Baltimore office who had been named a partner.

"There were more female partners at that party than there were women partners in the entire firm back in 1983. There are probably 15 female partners in the Washington area."

What's more, Hopkins contends that the down-and-dirty adversarial nature of the litigation process—which characterized her as a bitch who subjected underlings to verbal harangues—mischaracterized the partners' view of her the same way it has mischaracterized her.

"The litigation process polarizes. I am not what I have been characterized as in the newspapers and in the litigation process. I don't even recognize myself and people who know me don't recognize me at all. Nor in general would you recognize Price Waterhouse."

She has been back at Price Waterhouse since February 1991 and Hopkins says the work environment is "just fine. People in general have been incredibly supportive. All kinds of people have made all kinds of positive and congratulatory remarks to me, members of both sexes."

For all her bravado, however, Hopkins admits privately that the twists and turns of the case over more than six years have taken an emotional toll. "My kids would keep asking me how many times we have to win this case before it's over."[59]

For that reason, she counsels others who would follow in her footsteps to weigh all the issues before considering a lawsuit as a remedy for workplace inequities.

She's accustomed to giving advice because she fields several phone calls a month from women who have read about her case. "I probably take a couple of people to lunch each month who are considering suing somebody for something.

"I remember talking to a woman who worked for the federal government who was thinking about bringing a lawsuit over being passed over for a promotion from a GS12 to a GS13. I told her she has to decide whether the stakes involved make it worth the effort. She might be better off pursuing administrative remedies and having somebody get his hands slapped because I'm not sure a lawsuit is worth it. It may not be worth it in terms of the toll it'll take on you, the toll it will take on your family, and the amount of nervous stress you'll have to bear for the period of time you're going to have to bear it."

Choosing Another Alternative: Working For An Enlightened Organization

Hopkins believes that whether as a result of the lawsuit or just changing times, companies are finally coming around to the realization that they ought to recognize female talent within their employ. She cites the relatively enlightened attitude of the World Bank, an institution she worked for as a Budget Planner while waiting to be reinstated at Price Waterhouse.

"This is an international organization whose offices are located for all legal purposes 60 miles offshore of the United States and therefore not bound by the laws governing the United States. It's run by an international board of which not very many people give much of a damn about the role of women in the organization. However, the World Bank has a policy that in any instance where you've got a list of candidates for a management position in which a woman is shortlisted but not selected, the manager making the decision has to justify it. The World Bank has this policy despite having no incentive to give a bean about those kinds of issues."

No incentive? Maybe—or maybe this raised consciousness has something to do with a former female employee, Nancy Barry, who is currently President of Women's World Banking, which assists female entrepreneurs in developing countries.

Barry, one of the World Bank's few female Division Managers before she left in August 1990, had as one of her responsibilities compiling a report on the status of women at the bank. Among other things, the report showed that only 15 percent of its professional staff were women, a figure that had remained static since 1980. Barry says the president of the World Bank was "mortified" at her findings and at the end of 1988 implemented an action plan to recruit and promote women.

Barry confirmed that the very promotion policy Hopkins praised was a direct result of Barry's efforts at the bank. "There is definite causality there," she chuckled.

So it goes to show you that it only takes a few good women to make it better for other women in the workplace—one woman at a time.

chapter 17

FILING A LAWSUIT ON THE BASIS OF SEX DISCRIMINATION

Elizabeth Layman was 41 years old when Xerox Corp. eliminated her $60,000-a-year job as Marketing Manager in the company's Dallas office. Layman, a Xerox employee for seven years, had been promised a transfer to California. But after she sold her home and made other preparations to move, Xerox reneged on the offer.

While it moved younger male coworkers to other desirable jobs, the company assigned Layman to a spot for which she was overqualified. When her efforts to remedy the problem proved futile, she filed a suit against Xerox, alleging sex and age discrimination and other claims.

Six years after the trouble began, Layman won a jury verdict of more than $9 million. Her fight continues, however, since Xerox has challenged the verdict and made a motion for a new trial.

So not only does Layman have no money yet but she's spent plenty of her own, not to mention having her private life disrupted.

"There's nothing in my personal or work life that's not part of the public record," said Layman, who was on the witness stand for more than two weeks.[60]

As Layman—and Ann Hopkins—illustrate, lawsuits take their toll emotionally and literally. Before they're through, employees may have spent tens or even hundreds of thousands of dollars in lawyer's fees, recoverable only after a victory—if even then.

They must also cope with the emotional ups and downs of litigation, retaliation by employers (which may also be the basis of a legal claim) and the isolation that comes from being labeled a troublemaker. But if you have a case and want to pursue it, here's what you need to know.

Hitting Them Where They Live

Is it worth it to choose to fight—rather than switch, as Ann Hopkins did? From all appearances, Congress made life a little easier for victims of sex discrimination in the fall of 1991 when it enacted a civil rights bill that enabled them to receive jury awards for punitive damages, as opposed to mere compensatory damages that are intended to reimburse a plaintiff for injuries or harm—in other words, lost wages and out-of-pocket expenses. Previously, victims could only be awarded punitive damages in state courts in those states with statutes that allow it.

Under the new law, the ceiling on awards varies according to the size of the company, or, some might say, the depth of its pockets: up to $300,000 if you work for a company with more than 500 employees; up to $200,000 from a company that has between 201 and 500 employees; up to $100,000 if the company has between 101 and 200 employees, and up to $50,000 if the company has between 15 and 100 employees. Companies with fewer than 15 employees are exempt.

While business groups had contended that the law will result in a litigation explosion, this is highly unlikely. For one thing, most states in the north and far west already have laws on the books that permit jury awards. And women's advocates point to the likelihood the courts will continue to decide in favor of the defendants—the employers—if past is prologue. A study commissioned by the National Women's Law Center showed that plaintiffs only won 20 percent of 576 employment discrimination cases between 1980 and 1990. Furthermore, in nearly half the cases won by plaintiffs they didn't receive any damages;

even when damages were awarded only three of the plaintiffs got more than $200,000.[61]

Not surprisingly, lawyers who represent aggrieved employees generally support the Civil Rights Act, believing that companies have to be punished severely enough that they "cry Uncle" before they will start treating people fairly on the job. At least that's the view of Detroit attorney Kathleen Bogas.

"Because money means so much in this country, you have to make it too expensive for the employer not to change," Bogas said.

Tough antidiscrimination laws wield the same corrective clout that product liability law did, Bogas avers. "The only reason why we have seat belts or airbags in cars, the only reason why we have protectors on (industrial) presses for people who work on the assembly line is because it was costing the manufacturer of those goods too much money" from lawsuits from injured people.

Bogas says that drastic measures must be taken to counter the proemployer bias on the part of judges that has prevailed since the advent of the Reagan Administration. "It used to be that an attorney could make a prima facie case for any type of discrimination by showing that I, a female, got passed over for a promotion and a white male got the job."

But recent regressive Supreme Court decisions, including one that forbids the use of statistical evidence alone to show discrimination in the workplace, have rippled down through various lower federal courts and state courts.

Will the new federal law make the workplace more fair for women, by virtue of the fact that companies will have to fork out if they violate the law, or will it just mean a bonanza for attorneys who represent employees in discrimination cases?

John Rapoport, a Manhattan employee-rights attorney with his own practice, says yes and yes. "Yes, more employees will sue. And because of the additional damages under the federal act, more lawyers will probably be willing to take those cases. But more importantly, more employers will start managing more effectively within the law. It creates more incentive for management to understand what the law is."

Moreover, he adds, progressive laws beget more progressive laws.

"The city of New York just passed a new human rights law,

among the toughest in the country. I predict you'll see a continuation of the process of states and municipalities creating their own legislation that will continue to go one step beyond the federal government."

But Washington, D.C. employee-rights attorney James Heller sees a darker side, fearing that a weak economy could pose a greater threat to job security than unenlightened bosses, since minorities and women are most likely to be placed in jobs that are considered ballast when it's time to lighten the employee load.

"Business cutbacks are not good for women," said Heller, a partner in the Washington, D.C. firm of Kator, Scott & Heller, which handled Ann Hopkins' case. "They are among the last to rise to senior levels and their jobs will probably be among the first to be eliminated if there are cutbacks. Secondly, women tend to get fewer of the line jobs in industry, the jobs that would be the last to be cut. Women don't run assembly lines as often as they end up in human resources or some marketing specialty where management is much more likely to decide to combine two jobs into one or eliminate the job.

"Finally, since they aren't part of the old-boy club, the informal network, women are the least likely to be protected when cuts happen.

"So, while the law will do a lot to warn companies about the consequences of certain actions, it will not as clearly warn them about which employees should be saved. Those women who have most recently become successful will be most vulnerable to becoming victims of neutral forces. So I think there's not just a glass ceiling for women but there's a collapsible floor."

To Sue Or Not To Sue: Proving Company-Wide Discrimination

While the new civil rights law creates more opportunities for a woman to get compensation for her suffering, it doesn't relax the rules for proving sex discrimination, lower the cost of bringing a lawsuit, or mitigate the emotional cost of undergoing a trial.

The first thing you've got to do is prove that your case isn't just airtight, it's hermetically sealed. Because while you may think you have a discrimination case, the judge may just say you merely experienced the misfortune of working for a jerk.

While you don't have to prove that all other women in the office were treated as badly as yourself, it probably helps, says Joseph Golden, an attorney who is a partner in the Southfield, Michigan firm of Sommers, Schwartz, Silver & Schwartz.

"Usually the main defense that an employer uses is, 'Look, these (other) women were promoted; it's a matter of the qualifications of the individual.' Or they say the complaint isn't justifiably discrimination, it's got nothing to do with race and sex—it's a 'personality conflict' between the woman and her boss. We hear that all the time. And of course that plays well with the jury because anybody who's ever worked for anybody else knows that there's plenty of those conflicts in the workplace."

The more specifics you can offer to demonstrate that other women besides yourself were treated differently than men, the better off you are, agrees Washington, D.C. attorney James H. Heller.

Heller gave an example of some of the specifics: "Did people at the company say outright 'smoking gun' sexist things (about women employees)? And were these the people in power? How were pregnancies handled at the company? How were maternity leaves handled? What can you find out about numbers (instances of other women not getting promoted) and why aren't they getting ahead? Are women getting 'juniored' to men all the time?"

Filing a Sex Discrimination Complaint

Before you sue you must file a claim with the Federal Equal Employment Opportunity Commission, which enforces Title VII of the 1964 Civil Rights Act prohibiting discrimination in hiring, firing, wages, fringe benefits, promotion, or training. The function of the EEOC is to act as a mediator, ensuring that the aggrieved individual has exhausted her administration remedies and that she has a genuine case.[62]

If you decide to go the EEOC route, you must file a complaint generally within 300 days of the action you're protesting. If your state has a fair employment practice law, as 42 states do, your complaint may be sent to the state agency first.

If the state doesn't complete action on the complaint within 60 days, the EEOC may proceed to investigate the charge. The EEOC after its investigation makes a determination on the issue of "reasonable cause" as to discrimination. If there is reasonable cause, the agency makes its findings known to the employer and sees if the matter can be resolved. If that's not possible, the next step is a court suit.

Not surprisingly, the EEOC is as clogged with grievances, if not more, than the court system and in virtually every case the agency will issue you a "right to sue" letter. Once you receive the letter you have 90 days to file a court complaint.

Why bother to hire a lawyer if you can have the EEOC represent you for nothing? For one thing, like any federal bureaucracy, the EEOC may have its heart in the right place but it is understaffed and overworked, say attorneys. Attests Penny Nathan Kahan, a lawyer with her own practice in Chicago: "The EEOC is not an effective tool. They're overloaded and they don't put the time in that they should."

New York attorney John D. Rapoport rarely deals with the EEOC. "The (EEOC is) just too busy. They've got an enormous caseload; I've seen them turn people away who then came to me and they turned out to have a great case."

Before You Sue: Factors to Consider

Before you decide to sue, ask yourself whether you can afford to lose the case. Lawyers don't come cheap; depending on your geographic location, their fees range from $75 per hour to $350-plus an hour and few attorneys will handle your case on a strict contingency basis unless you've got an airtight case; i.e., in which case you win and the defendant winds up paying your attorney fees. Just paying court stenographers to prepare deposition transcripts can run $1,000 a day.

Says attorney Maryann Saccomando Freedman of the Buffalo firm of Lavin and Kleiman, "Meeting the burden of proof is tough to begin with in a sex discrimination case, it's going to be difficult to prove. And along with that you're going to have to lay out all this money and you may lose the case. That's a very serious concern because most women are not earning that much money to be able to pick up that tab."

The second question to ask yourself is why are you suing. Do you want your old job back, or the promotion you should have had, or money: restitution for lost salary and monetary damages for the psychological toll. This is the most important question to weigh and the answer will vary depending on your circumstances.

The reinstatement option isn't usually advised, says Kathleen Bogas of the Detroit law firm of Sachs, Nunn, Kates, Kadushian, O'Hare, Helveston, and Waldman.

"Very seldom do I represent somebody who is currently in a job and suing somebody for discriminatory practices," Bogas said. "I don't encourage people to file suit while they're still working there."

Why? Even if your old boss doesn't try to buy you off, getting your old job back—or even winning the promotion you deserved—is usually a psychologically devastating experience to the worker. Because you're really returning to the scene of the crime, as it were.

"It's psychologically damaging for people," Bogas said. "(The woman is) going to be looking over her shoulder constantly. If somebody doesn't say good morning to her in the morning she's going to think they didn't because she brought the lawsuit. You can't help it, it's a natural human reaction."

When a client insists she wants reinstatement, Bogas counsels her to analyze the emotional turmoil she's experiencing, which is not unlike being spurned by a lover and wanting him back.

"If they do (say they want reinstatement) when they first see me I say to them, 'Are you crazy? Why do you want to go back and work there? The best thing that could happen to you is that you got fired or left.'

"They come to realize that. But in an employment case you experience a variety of emotions—you go through anger, you go through hate and then at the end you say, 'You know, I'm just going to get what's mine.'

"And a lot of people unfortunately latch onto these cases and won't give up on them and live their lives and do everything for the case. And that's the worst thing you can do. I don't know if life is worth it."

For one thing, Chicago attorney Penny Nathan Kahan points out that even if you win the promotion you deserved that doesn't mean you've achieved the "right" to continued career success at the company. Kahan can point to only one instance in her practice in which she was satisfied that her client's prospects were going to improve; in that case she was able to create a mentor system to assist in the woman's career climb.

What's more, Kahan says, even if you decide to pursue your career at a different company, your ability to get a job elsewhere may be tainted if people brand you as a troublemaker.

"If you're in a narrow field there's a strong grapevine" that could backfire if you tried to get another job, Kahan said.

John Poynton, an outplacement counselor with the Executive Assets Corp. in Chicago, agrees: "Corporations will hesitate to hire someone who's initiated an action." What's more, he said, the time and energy you spend on a lawsuit rather than on job-hunting, "directly lengthens the job search."[63]

If You Quit: Proving Your Case

If you do decide to quit your job and sue your former employer, you may have to demonstrate to a skeptical judge that staying in the old job would have produced undue stress or that the company essentially "terminated" your career, says New York attorney John Rapoport.

This is called *constructive termination* says Rapoport, who is the author of *The Employee Strikes Back* (Macmillan, 1989). "Does the fact that you were passed over give you the right to quit?" Rapoport contends that in passing you over your employer was "really firing you, they just didn't say the words."

That was the argument of the attorneys for management consultant Ann Hopkins, who wasn't just pushed off the ladder but deprived of the top rung. In that case, not getting the job was perhaps more injurious to her career than fighting to get it back.

"When you're being considered for a partnership in accounting firms and law firms it's usually 'up or out'; once you're not made partner you're out," said Rapoport. "And that has a lot of other stigmas attached to it because everybody knows you were up for partner. It significantly alters your ability to do your job when you're passed over."

But an individual who is a candidate for the partnership is a far cry from somebody who's "working for XYZ company who wants to be the Assistant Manager of widgets and they hire somebody else to do it instead," Rapoport said. "Not everybody passed up for advancement has the absolute right to a golden-parachute lawsuit."

While Rapoport agrees that staying at your old employer is "nuts most of the time," there are certain circumstances when it's worth fighting for. "If it turns out to be the greatest place I ever worked—I loved everybody there and they all loved me—but because some old fogey SOB didn't like women I didn't get promoted, don't you dare come to me and tell me I can't sue!"

On the other hand, "you don't have to go back. You can just take the back pay and other damages—in a state court suit you might get punitive damages too. Take them and run."

But aren't we now just talking about pure gut revenge against the company, as opposed to rectifying an unjust situation? Absolutely not, Rapoport avers. "It's no more revenge than if you fall down a flight of stairs because somebody consistently leaves a banana peel there and you sue for personal injury. You had a peronal injury done to you."

Know the Laws that Protect Working Women from Sex Discrimination

Needless to say, being passed over for a promotion is only one of many ways women confront on-the-job discrimination. Employers sometimes try to get away with paying women less than men doing the same job, or they'll claim certain jobs aren't appropriate for women or they'll say that a woman who has left for a maternity leave has rescinded the right to have her old job back.

The next sections provide a brief summary of many of the important laws that protect working women.

THE PREGNANCY DISCRIMINATION ACT AND MATERNITY LEAVE LAWS

As recently as the 1970s, some employers weren't even keen on letting women work while they were pregnant, much less after they had attained Mom status.

In LaFleur v. Cleveland Board of Education (1974), female public school teachers successfully challenged the constitutionality of mandatory maternity leave rules of the Cleveland, Ohio and Chesterfield County, Virginia school boards.[64]

Among the policies being challenged was the Cleveland School Board's policy requiring pregnant teachers to take leave five months before the expected date of birth, presumably because that's when a woman starts "showing," and to continue on leave until the beginning of the next regular semester following the date of the child's three-month birthday.

The Supreme Court held that the policy created an "irrebutable" presumption that all pregnant teachers are disabled and thus unfit to teach, penalizing the teachers for exercising their fundamental right to decide whether or not to bear a child.

Have we come a long way, baby, when it comes to having babies? The laws have improved but corporate practices in general have not.

The Pregnancy Discrimination Act was added to Title VII in 1978 to prohibit discrimination on the basis of pregnancy, childbirth, or related conditions.

But the law doesn't say anything about getting your old job back when your maternity leave is over. In 1983 news anchor Mary Loftus was fired from her job at KSNT-TV the day she came home from the hospital after giving birth to her son.[65]

Although she was able to get a job at a competing station, she started at the bottom again, for half her former pay. "The economic loss was substantial," she said. "And I took a giant step backward careerwise."

The United States is one of only two industrialized countries—the other one being South Africa—that fails to ensure that a woman can return to her job after taking time off to have a child, says Sally F. Goldfarb, staff attorney for the National Organization for Women Legal Defense and Education Fund.[66] A federal bill that would provide workers unpaid leave to care for new babies or sick parents was vetoed by President George Bush in 1990 and again in 1991.

Recent research indicates that maternity leaves are taken at a woman's own risk.

Wright State University researchers William Schoemaerk and Ann Wendt, who studied 2,000 employment discrimination claims between 1985 and 1989, say 23 percent of women who took maternity leave weren't rehired, compared to 2 percent of women who took leaves for other reasons.[67]

In one case, a social worker found her belongings packed in boxes when she returned to work. Another, who had ironically enough taken over the job of a pregnant secretary, lost her own job four years later when she tried to return from maternity leave.

But Title VII does offer some job protection to women who want to work and have babies. Here are some of the provisos:

- A company can't refuse to hire a woman because she is pregnant.

- An employer can't fire a woman because she is pregnant.

- It's illegal to force a pregnant woman to leave her job if she is ready, willing, and able to perform.

- If a pregnancy prevents a woman from performing certain tasks—for example, heavy lifting—she must be given alternate assignments.

- The seniority process can't be delayed for an employee who has taken a leave to give birth or have an abortion unless seniority is similarly delayed for other disabled people. That goes for calculating vacation time and pay increases as well.

- Companies can't require pregnant workers to exhaust their vacation benefits before receiving sick pay or disability benefits unless all temporarily disabled employees are required to do the same.

- Pregnancy-related expenses should be reimbursed in the same manner as are expenses for any other medical condition.

- An employer can't have a rule that mandates a minimum duration of maternity leave.

- If an employer has a policy that permits people to take a leave of absence without pay for travel to further their education that isn't job related, the same leave must be available for those who want to extend their maternity leave, even if the person is medically able to work.

- Unless the employee has informed the employer that she doesn't intend to return to work, her job must be held open on the same basis as jobs are held open for employees on sick or disability leave or for other reasons.

Read that last one carefully—this proviso does not mean a company has to have a maternity leave policy, it only means that if the company has a disability policy, it has to treat pregnant disabled workers the same as other kinds of disabled workers.

If your company doesn't have a disability policy that protects the jobs of temporarily disabled workers or a specific maternity leave provision, "there isn't anything they have to do," says Michigan attorney Joseph Golden. "They'll say we'll give you your old job back 'if it's available' or something similar 'if it's available'—and of course they fill it.

"You can't do anything about it unless you can show that in circumstances where men who were off the job under similar conditions—if a man broke his arm, for example—the company did not move to replace the man quickly as they did with the women."

About 25 states have some form of family leave protection, according to Donna Lenhoff, legal director of the Women's Legal Defense Fund in Washington.[68]

The New York State Human Rights Law prohibits employment discrimination by employers with four or more workers on the basis of pregnancy, childbirth, or related conditions. New York state employers can't compel a pregnant employee to take a leave of absence unless the pregnancy prevents satisfactory job performance. New York also has a mandatory disability law so employees on pregnancy leave are entitled to disability benefits.

JOB DISCRIMINATION BASED ON GENDER

As we mentioned earlier in the chapter, Title VII of the Civil Rights Act of 1964 prohibits discrimination based on race, sex, color, religion, or national origin.

Among its strictures:

- Help wanted ads can't discriminate based on gender unless gender is a bona fide occupational qualification for the job involved. (Needless to say, outside of jock strap modeling jobs, there ain't a heckuva lot of bona fide excuses for not considering a female candidate.)

- Prospective employers can't ask you a question on a job interview which expresses limitation or discrimination as to gender unless it's based on a bona fide occupational qualification.
- Employers can't forbid or restrict the employment of married women unless they do the same to married men.
- Employers can't qualify a job as male or female, maintain separate sex-based lines of progression or seniority requirements unless gender is a bona fide occupational qualification for the job.

Some states go further. California laws protect employees' jobs when they marry so that each partner must be allowed to retain the job (Compare this to Hopkins' experience with Touche Ross.) In some cases, these laws have been interpreted to cover married couples who work for competing companies.

Within California, the cities of Los Angeles and San Francisco prohibit discrimination or discharge on the basis of sexual preference or orientation.

EQUAL PAY

The Equal Pay Act of 1963 was the first federal law designed to prevent sex discrimination by forbidding unequal pay for women and men who work in the same establishment in the same or similar jobs; that is, jobs which require equal skill, effort, and responsibility.

Pay also refers to overtime, uniforms, and travel. Nor can companies treat men and women doing the same work differently in offering fringe benefits, including pension and retirement plans.

Employers can't claim that the cost of employing women is greater—because of time off from the job having babies, and so forth—in order to get away with paying them less. What's more, it's illegal to pay a woman less than a man because she's allegedly not the head of the household. Remember Shirley Prutch's story. At least we've made progress.

chapter 18

EPILOGUE: 16 WAYS TO MAKE THE WORKPLACE WORK FOR YOU

Remarking on the career of Katharine Hepburn, *New York Times* columnist Anna Quindlen observed that the most lasting contribution the legendary actress has made to womankind has been to legitimize self-centeredness as a female character trait.[69]

"The selfless self has always been the rage in women," Quindlen writes. "Hepburn was something else again, with her bold and unapologetic self-center."

Katharine Hepburn established that a woman can be fulfilled if she chooses a career instead of kids, that it's okay to wear pants even if everybody else of your gender is wearing a dress—who wants to cross their legs, anyway? And it's okay to prefer an affair with the man you love to marriage to a man you don't.

For working women, this self-centeredness takes on a specific meaning: it's okay to insist on the job, the boss, the company, and the respect you deserve. It's okay to cultivate allies, scheme for promotions, and otherwise "be aggressive" rather than wait to be asked to the dance. Even if you have to raise your voice, make a stink, defy tradition, and do other "unladylike" things. Conversely, it's okay to want to find satisfaction in a smaller company or by getting on a "slower track" in human resources or some other staff function, even though convention may dictate that success is defined as power in a line job or in a "name" corporation.

What derails career women more than anything else is—

and here I go, stereotyping like I hate other people to—their tendency to live by somebody else's yardstick. This makes them more likely to take career setbacks personally instead of assuming that you can't please all of your bosses all of the time, especially those bosses who are threatened by competent, intelligent women. Women should learn to be self-centered, and that's not the same as selfish, in the workplace. Because the workplace is lucky to have them.

To get women started on a self-centered approach to their careers, here are 16 tips on how to make the workplace work for you:

1. **Work at a job you love.** Then it won't be difficult to be terrific at it. Sara Westendorf shelved a career in social work for one in engineering because she decided she'd rather be paid well to solve problems than eke out a starvation wage never solving them.

2. **Work at a company that loves you.** It may sound more prestigious and more impressive on paper to be a big frog in a big pond, but smaller is often better when you can't stomach corporate politics. As Nancy Faunce and Melissa Cadet point out, you're more visible to the powers that be and you're more likely to get ahead on merit.

3. **Work at a job that loves you.** Chapter 15's Barbara Williams discovered after she was turned down for a leadership track job that her public relations job wasn't so bad after all; it afforded her intellectual stimulation through writing and travel as opposed to a fast-track job where she'd spend more time playing politics than being productive.

4. Except in rare circumstances, **don't be put in a subordinate, secretarial position.** As a minority, Melissa Cadet carries out a mission to "reprogram" those male minds who accept by default the notion of minorities as second-class citizens. The same reprogramming process must occur with those men who believe that women should be barefoot, pregnant, or taking dictation.

   For example, if you're in a meeting and a male peer or outsider who doesn't have a grasp of your authority or position asks you to take notes, use Melissa Cadet's "diplomatic confrontationalist" approach: suggest that somebody else do it or get a secretary. Sure, you don't want to be written off as an ill-tempered feminist but you don't want to be mistaken for a doormat, either.

5. **Work smart.** Don't be surprised if you have to prove yourself to male clients or suppliers or even potential collaborators within your company who aren't aware of your authority. Preempt skepticism by conveying the message that you're an "insider" to the process. This often means overwhelming the individuals with technical jargon—"authority words"—specific to your responsibilities, as does Karen Reimer when conversing with acquisition candidates and as Sara Westendorf does when attempting to do joint work with lab managers in other parts of the country.

6. **Be realistic.** Face facts, as Karen Reimer does, that you "can't remake the world in a moment" and transform entrenched views about women in the workplace overnight. There will be situations in which you've got to stay in the background on a deal if it means that your presence might otherwise throw a monkeywrench into it. Sara Westendorf also has come to terms with the fact that the members of her engineering team have to prove themselves on their diagnostic work for Japanese automakers before she dares show her face in their presence for fear of scotching the deal. And, even as Honeywell's director of corporate transactions, Reimer often has to send in male lawyers to convey her negotiating strategy to a "buy" or "sell" candidate because the men on the other side of the table often don't "hear" ultimatums from women.

7. **Don't take "maybe later" for an answer** if you're up for a promotion you deserve and you're turned down or if you're already in a management position and you aren't given the tools to do your job. Because "maybe" really means "no."

   When the California agriculture department told Melissa Cadet she wasn't ready for a promotion after five years of outstanding results, she hit the pavement rather than wait for Godot. When Cadet's aerospace employer told her to "work around" an incompetent secretary instead of allowing her to replace the woman, she left for an employer who took her seriously. When Jacquie Arthur couldn't satisfy herself that she'd end up on the fast track at Avery

Dennison, she turned down an otherwise generous offer and impressive title and opted for an employer who gave her a better shot at the driver's seat.

8. **Be suspicious of a boss that patronizes you.** Chapter 15's Jeanne Rice traded her corporate employee job for a free-lance writing job after getting fed up with being treated like a "corporate daughter"; having a boss react to her brilliant presentation by rhapsodizing about her "cute-ness." Judy Frank wasted time working for a boss who decided to mother her once she became a mother and wouldn't let her work late hours. While at first glance this behavior doesn't seem offensive, just pathetic, it's merely a benign form of discrimination—these guys like you just fine, they just don't respect you.

9. **Make sure your husband supports your work.** It's vir-tually impossible for a woman to demand that her col-leagues, underlings, and superiors take her seriously if her husband won't. A solid marriage is one that is based on teamwork: mutual respect and mutual career support. And teamwork means that the male member of the team is not permitted to assume that the female member is going to fulfill the role of chief cook and bottlewasher along with that of being a full-time wage-earner. If both members of a couple are working 9 to 5 or 9 to 9, a working woman's other half either has to pitch in and help with housework, cooking, and the kids, or agree to pay for outside help.

10. **Don't be naive and assume that somebody at work is going to look out for you.** No, there is no Santa Claus and there are no guardian angels. Frequently women dupe themselves into the fantasy that because the federal and local laws dictate fairness in the workplace, at least in the areas of sex discrimination, that everybody in the work-place is going to play by them. Naturally, no woman should walk around with a chip on her shoulder expecting to be sabotaged, but don't expect to be "taken care of" either.

11. **Lighten up and have fun.** If the guys are going out for a drink, join them. Take your customers out, too. (Sure, men hate it when women pick up the tab but just tell them your boss would be suspicious if you didn't pay the bill.)

12. **Know the signs of discrimination.** Your boss won't ever come out and say, "we're passing you over for a job because you are a woman," he'll tell you instead, "You're not ready yet for management." Your subordinate won't tell you straight out, "I won't work for you because you are a woman," instead he'll question your credentials. Or, resentful subordinates will manifest their lack of respect by throwing the grownup equivalent of a temper tantrum and not turn their work in.

13. **Don't take recalcitrant subordinates personally.** If you've got a male subordinate who resents working for you because you're a woman, that's his problem. Unfortunately, in many circumstances, the laws dictating fair play are more enlightened than the people who have to obey them, including Title VII of the Civil Rights Act that says that men and women are equally capable of doing a job. The law defends your rights—and your boss must defend your authority—not the resentful subordinate's attitude.

    Sure, you can use "diplomatic confrontation," as Melissa Cadet does, to get employees to open up about their feelings. But recognize, as Linda Wroblewski does, that you run the ballfield. You're there to get a job done and if their resentment compromises their business goals, your subordinates have to find a new attitude or a new boss.

14. **Don't take failures personally.** Don't be surprised if nobody at work loves you when you're down and out. If you fall from grace at work, as Nancy Faunce did, and you discover that your erstwhile best buddies now treat you as if you had leprosy, click your heels three times and say to yourself, "They're the problem, not me."

    More important, don't let bad bosses define your self-esteem. Judy Frank and Nancy Faunce both admit they wasted valuable emotional energy blaming themselves for career setbacks instead of chalking up the experience to experience, as men seem to be able to do with more finesse. Like it or not, perhaps the experience men gain in competitive team sports serves some useful purpose after all because it teaches them how to lose as well as win.

    Author Betty Lehan Harragan says that team members take defeat in stride, evaluating it as a lesson in life, not a failing grade on their personal report card. "Mothers of Little League boys fondly reminisce about the days when a team defeat desolated their child as if the world had ended . . . (Her son) will not comprehend that his mother has been denied a similar growth opportunity, that she is still at the Little League starting gate, personally feeling demolished, distraught, and disconcerted by any little imperfection, rebuff, blunder, or awkwardness."[70]

15. **Help other women get into management,** or just plain help them by being a friend. Melissa Cadet does this by becoming the mentor she never had through her activities with the National Association for Female Executives. Jacquie Arthur did it at Dennison by serving on a diversity committee that tried to get more women and minorities into management. Karen Reimer does it by bringing women who are junior to her into meetings with the top brass where they can pitch their ideas and get noticed by the right people.

    Unfortunately, we working women have a reputation for, at best, looking out for Number One and forgetting everybody else, or, at worst, sabotaging the success of other women because we fear that their success jeopardizes our place in the pecking order. We need to realize that we're all in this together.

16. **Believe in yourself.** Nobody in this world achieved greatness in art, science, business, or any other discipline by second guessing what the power brokers thought of them. Measure your personal goals by your own yardstick and you'll find others more likely to measure theirs by yours.

ENDNOTES

Chapter 1: Women in Management

1. Roper survey on sex harassment is from "Sex Harassment Is not a Common Workplace Problem," *The Wall Street Journal*, March 24, 1992.

2. Melanie Kirkpatrick quote is from "Anita Hill's Victims," *The Wall Street Journal*, October 10, 1991.

3. Kathryn Gray quote is from "Anita Hill—Another Victim to Blame," *The Wall Street Journal*, October 24, 1991.

4. Lorraine Dusky quote is from "Don't Blame the Baby: Why Women Leave Corporations," by Wick and Co., 1990.

5. Frances Conley anecdote is from "Walking Out on the Boys," *Time*, July 8, 1991.

6. Lawsuit against Texaco is from "Woman Gets $6.3 Million in Sex-Bias Case," *The Wall Street Journal*, September 27, 1991.

7. Ingrid Beall anecdote is from "Bringing Suite Against Her Own Firm," *The New York Times*, October 13, 1991.

Chapter 2: So Near, Yet So Far

8. Statistics on female participation in certain professions and college enrollments are from "Onward, Women!," *Time*, December 4, 1989.

9. Statistics on college enrollment (see note 8).

10. Anecdote about female MBAs at Harvard in 1959 is from "Women on the Verge of Being CEO," *Business Month*, April 1990.

11. Statistics about female MBAs at Harvard, Stanford and Columbia are from "Topping Out," *Executive Female*, March/April, 1989.

12. *Fortune* magazine survey results from "Why Women Still Don't Hit the Top," *Fortune*, July 30, 1990.

13. Data on minority women and quote is from Ella Bell is from "Both Racism and Sexism Block the Path to Management for Minority Women," *The Wall Street Journal*, July 25, 1990.

14. Anecdote about "Black Enterprise" is from *The Wall Street Journal*, July 25, 1990.

15. Quote from Ella Bell (see note 14).

16. Anecdote about First Woman's Bank is from "Making a Women's Bank Balance," *Sunday (London) Times Magazine*, November 4, 1990.

17. American Bankers Association survey, *Los Angeles Times* survey and Pam Mollica quote from "Topping Out," *Executive Female*, March/April 1989.

18. *Los Angeles Times* survey (see note 17).

19. Pam Mollica quote (see note 17)

20. Patricia Jones anecdote (see note 17).

21. Financial Women International survey is from "Glass Ceiling Unseen—Unless You Hit Your Head," *The Wall Street Journal*, October 18, 1990.

22. Digiovacchino quote (see note 21).

23. Victoria Fung study is from "Women in Broadcast News," *Executive Female*, January/February 1989.

24. Menkel-Meadow study on law is from "Unequal Partners," *Executive Female*, January/February 1989.

25. American Bar Association survey results are from "Sex Bias Case Going Before Supreme Court," *New York Newsday*, October 9, 1988.

26. American Institute of Certified Public Accountants survey is from "Sex Bias Case Going Before Supreme Court."

27. Arthur Bowman quote is from "The Big Eight: Still a Male Bastion," *The New York Times*, July 12, 1988.

28. Data on Big Eight (see note 27).

29. Statistics on women in academia is from "Women in Waiting," *The New York Times* educational supplement, 1991.

30. Judy Mello quote is from "Why Women Still Don't Hit the Top."

31. Data on Business Week survey from "Corporate Women/ They're About to Break Through to the Top," *Business Week*, June 22, 1987.

32. Study by Wick & Co., is from "Women Managers Quit Not for Family but to Advance Their Corporate Climb," *The Wall Street Journal*, May 2, 1990.

33. Tashjian quote (see note 32).

34. Opinion Research Corp. study (see note 32).

35. Glass Ceiling data, Elizabeth Dole's quote is from "Labor Dept. Wants to Take on Job Bias in the Executive Suite," *The New York Times*, July 30, 1990.

36. Findings on glass-ceiling study and data from Office of Federal Contract Compliance are from "The Study That Makes it Official," *Working Woman*, October, 1991.

37. Marcia Greenberger quote is from "How Lynn Martin's Career Will Affect Yours," *Working Woman*, October, 1991.

38. Data on diverse workforce is from Bureau of Labor Statistics as cited in "Learning to Accept Cultural Diversity," *The Wall Street Journal*, September 12, 1990.

39. Harbridge House data on minority women's share of the workforce is from "Both Racism and Sexism Bock the Path . . ."

40. Kentucky Fried Chicken anecdote is from "PepsiCo's KFC Scouts for Blacks and Women for Its Top Echelons," *The Wall Street Journal*, November 13, 1991.

41. Chubb anecdotes are from "Women Managers Quit Not for Family . . ."

42. Corning anecdote is from "One Firm's Bid to Keep Blacks, Women," *The Wall Street Journal*, February 16, 1989.

43. Felice Schwartz quote is from "Trailblazer Now a Traitor?," *The Record*, March 20, 1990.

44. Janet Daly's observations are from "Still Belittled After 11 Years," *The (London) Independent*, November 21, 1990.

45. The Sadker study on college professors is from "Women on the Verge of an Education," *In View* (Whittle Communications), Vol. 2, Issue 4.

46. The Sadker study on schools is from "Sexism in Our Schools," *Better Homes and Gardens*, February 1981.

47. Florence Geis study is from "Studies Find Workplace Still a Man's World," *The Boston Globe*, March 12, 1990.

48. George Clement quote is from "Why Women Walk Out on Jobs," *The New York Times*, April 29, 1990.

Chapter 3: Why So Few Good Women?

49. Observations about immigrants is from *More Like Us*, James Fallows, Houghton Mifflin, 1989.

50. Observations about Californians (see note 49).

Chapter 12: Sara Levinson

51. Quotes on attending her high school reunion are from "What's the Big Idea," *Working Woman*, July 1990.

Chapter 15: Lessons from the Trenches

52. Jeanne Rice anecdote is from "When Fatherly Concern Isn't Welcome," *The Wall Street Journal Europe*, March 26, 1991.

53. Susan Cross anecdotes are from "Pregnant Employees in U.S. Still Encounter Discrimination Despite Legal Protection," *The Wall Street Journal Europe*, February 18, 1991.

54. Robin Piccone anecdote (see note 53).

55. Sara Corse study is from "Pregnant Managers and Their Subordinates: The Effects of Gender Expectations on Hierarchic Relationships," *The Journal of Applied Behavioral Science*, Vol. 26, No. 1.

Chapter 16: Ann Hopkins

56. "Movement person" quote is from " 'Social Grace' Care Raises Question of Subtle Sex Bias in Workplace," *The Washington Post*, Oct. 29, 1988.

57. Role model quote is from "Bucking the System," *The Miami Herald*, May 18, 1990.

58. Lynn Schafran quote (see note 57).

59. How many times to we have to win quote is from "Forget Charm School," *Boston Globe*, June 19, 1990.

Chapter 17: Filing a Lawsuit

60. Anecdote about Elizabeth Layman is from "The High Cost of Suing the Boss," *The (New York) Daily News*, June 3, 1990.

61. National Women's Law Center study is from "Fight Isn't Over As Job Bias Bill Goes to Bush," *The Wall Street Journal*, October 18, 1990.

62. Data on filing complaints with the EEOC is from *The State-by-State Guide to Women's Legal Rights*, by the NOW/Legal Defense and Education Fund and Renee Cherow-O'Leary, McGraw-Hill Book Co., 1987.

63. Quote from John Poynton is from "Getting Mad, Then Getting Even," *The New York Times*, July 1, 1990.

64. Description of LaFleur v. Cleveland Board of Education is from "Legal Resource Kit: Employment—Pregnancy and Parental Leave," *NOW Legal Defense and Education Fund* (undated).

65. Mary Loftus anecdote is from "Taking Time off for the Family," *The New York Times*, March 25, 1990.

66. Sally Goldfarb quote (see note 65).

67. Wright State University research is from "New Mothers Have Trouble Getting Their Jobs Back," *The Wall Street Journal*, August 20, 1991 and "Caution: Maternity Leave Taken At One's Own Risk," *The Wall Street Journal*, November 13, 1991.

68. Donna Lenhoff quote is from "Taking Time off for the Family," *The New York Times*, March 25, 1990.

Chapter 18: Epilogue

69. Quindlen quote is from "Reading Hepburn," *The New York Times*, October 23, 1991.

70. Little League quote is from *Games Mother Never Taught You*, by Betty Lehan Harragan, Warner Books, 1977.

INDEX